D1526062

The Mexican Legal System

THE
MEXICAN
LEGAL SYSTEM

FRANCISCO A. AVALOS

Reference Guides to National Legal Systems, Number 1

GREENWOOD PRESS
New York • Westport, Connecticut • London

Library of Congress Cataloging-in-Publication Data

Avalos, Francisco.
    The Mexican legal system / Francisco A. Avalos.
        p.   cm. — (Reference guides to national legal systems, ISSN
    1059-9134 ; no. 1)
    Includes bibliographical references and indexes.
    ISBN 0-313-27565-3 (alk. paper)
        1. Legal research — Mexico.   2. Law — Mexico — Indexes.   3. Law —
    Mexico — Bibliography.   I. Title.   II. Series.
    KGF150.A95   1992
    016.34972 — dc20
    [016.3472]   91-39512

British Library Cataloguing in Publication Data is available.

Library of Congress Catalog Card Number: 91-39512
ISBN: 0-313-27565-3
ISSN: 1059-9134

First published in 1992

Greenwood Press, 88 Post Road West, Westport, CT 06881
An imprint of Greenwood Publishing Group, Inc.

Printed in the United States of America

The paper used in this book complies with the
Permanent Paper Standard issued by the National
Information Standards Organization (Z39.48-1984).

10 9 8 7 6 5 4 3 2 1

This work is dedicated to

Kathleen Dolores

Contents

Preface

This work has been conceived and written to serve as a primary resource guide to the laws and legal literature of Mexico. It is designed to overcome problems facing the non-expert when dealing with Mexican legal research. The guide provides answers to the questions most frequently asked: "Which is the relevant code?"; "Where can the text of the code be found?"; "What secondary material is available?"; "Which of the material is available in English?"

Because of the importance of federal legislation over state legislation in Mexico, this guide concentrates primarily on federal legislation. The federal material is organized into forty-one subject sections. The subject headings used are patterned on the subject headings used by the Library of Congress. A broad, liberal interpretation of the subject headings is used; for example, under "Banks and Banking," all laws broadly associated with monetary and financial matters are included. Included under this heading are "The Organic Laws of the Bank of Mexico," "The Laws of Credit Institutions," "The Currency Laws," and others.

Each of the forty-one sections is further divided into four subsections. The first lists all of the laws for the subject. The official names of the laws are given, accompanied by the English translation of the names, followed by the date of publication of the laws in the "Diario Oficial" (Official Government Gazette). The second subsection lists sources for the text of the laws other than the "Diario Oficial," since the "Diario Oficial" is extremely difficult to locate. The third subsection lists periodical literature relating to the subject. The fourth subsection lists all books and monographs relating to the subject. All Spanish-language sources listed have their titles translated into English. English- language primary and secondary materials have been especially sought out and included in the guide.

The guide concludes with a section on state materials, with no subject breakdown. Only references to primary materials are listed for the State legislation.

Although the guide is comprehensive, it is not all inclusive. State primary materials are especially selective. A general index is provided. English-language primary and secondary sources have been emphasized in this index.

Acknowledgments

I offer my gratitude to the members of the University of Arizona College of Law Library staff. Specifically to Ronald L. Cherry for his patience, encouragement and support throughout the course of this project.

I am also grateful to Boris Kozolchyk, who in many ways has made this work possible. And finally to Anne Kathleen for her invaluable help and understanding.

The Mexican Legal System

Introduction

Today's legal system of Mexico is the result
of the dynamics of many unique social, racial,
political,religious,   economical,   and
historical factors that gave birth to the
Mexican nation and that have propelled it to
the present. An exhaustive study of such a
complex social institution is far beyond the
scope of this work. This work, as the title
implies, is a guide to the legal system of
Mexico. It is meant to serve as the point of
departure for the study of the legal system of
Mexico and not as the final point for such a
study. The guide is arranged by legal topic
and points to primary and secondary sources.
Primary and secondary English-language sources
were sought out especially for inclusion in
this guide.

   The Mexican legal system has historical
roots that go back to 16th-century Spanish law
and to Pre-Columbian indigenous law.[1] Spain
ruled Mexico for over three hundred years and
consequently left its mark on the legal system
of Mexico. The link to Pre-Columbian
indigenous law is traced through the Aztec
Empire, which was the dominant political power
in Mexico at the time of the arrival of the
Spaniards. The Spanish conquistadores found an
advanced indigenous legal system in place when

they conquered the Aztec Empire.[2] The Spanish
Crown did not do away completely with the
indigenous legal system. Instead, the Crown
kept the indigenous laws and legal
institutions that did not go directly against
established Spanish customs or against Church
doctrine.[3] The Spanish Crown also introduced
its own laws and legal institutions to replace
and/or supplement what was discarded, and the
Crown passed laws and created legal
institutions that were intended for Colonial
Mexico, legislation that did not exist in
Spain.[4]

For the next three hundred years "Spanish
law was the dominant feature in the Mexican
legal" system.[5] Spanish law was most dominant
in the area of private law; in matters of
commerce, property, family inheritance, and
obligations, Spanish law was used almost
exclusively.[6] In the area of public law,
indigenous law and the law that was passed
exclusively for Colonial Mexico "was very
comprehensive and it was the major source of
the law for Colonial Mexico".[7] There were
several attempts made to place together in a
single code all of the laws pertaining to
Colonial Mexico. The results of these efforts
were the "Cedula de Puga (1556, Decrees and
Orders of Puga)," "Nueva Recopilacion (1567,
New Compilation)," "Codigo Ovandino (1571,
Ovandino Code)," "Recopilacion de Leyes de las
Indias (1680, Compilation of the Laws of the
Indies)," and "Novisima Recopilacion (1805,
Newest Compilation)."[8] Another important
compilation of laws of the period was the
"Ordenanzas de Bilboa (1737, Statutes of
Bilboa)." This code concerned private law
matters and "became the commercial code and
was used in Mexico even after Independence."[9]

The movement towards Mexican Independence started in 1810. In 1814 the Constitution of Apatzingan was issued.[10] Although this constitution never came into effect, many "ideas it expressed served as a model for future changes".[11] The Apatzingan Constitution incorporated secular natural law and secular positive law which were the product of the revolutions that took place in the Western world in the eighteenth and nineteenth centuries beginning with the American Revolution. The crux of secular natural law and secular postive law is that all individuals are created equal with natural rights to property, to liberty, and to life. It is the responsibility of the government, which should be divided into separate, independent powers, to recognize and secure these rights for the individual.[12] The American Declaration of Independence and the French Declaration of the Rights of Man and of the Citizen are prime examples of the new eighteenth- and nineteenth-century political philosophy. Nationalistic fervor also formed part of the new political philosophy.

Mexico achieved independence in 1821 and adopted its first constitution in 1824.[13] The 1824 Constitution provided for a Federal Republic consisting of nineteen states, four territories, and a Federal District. The 1824 Constitution also provided for recognition of self-determination; division of power into the executive, the legislative, and the judiciary; the equality of all citizens before the law; the principle of innocent until proven guilty; freedom of expression and of the press; the protection of private property; the abolition of special privileges for the clergy and the military; and agrarian reform.

The 1824 Constitution was never applied strictly because of internal armed conflict between the conservative and liberal elements of the newly independent Mexican nation. In 1857 a new constitution was adopted, which was drafted by the liberal elements who had ascended to power.[14] The most important contribution of the 1857 Constitution was the writ of "amparo" (see pages 12-13 for an explanation of the writ of "amparo").[15] The 1857 Constitution survived a civil war and the French intervention of 1862. It was not until after the triumph of the 1910 Mexican Revolution that the 1857 Constitution was replaced by the current Mexican Constitution of 1917.

The current Mexican Constitution is commonly referred to as the 1917 Constitution. The official name of this Constitution is the Political Constitution of the United Mexican States (Constitucion Politica de los Estados Unidos Mexicanos). The original name given to this constitution was the Political Constitution of the United Mexican States, that revises the one of February 5 of 1857 (Constitucion Politica de los Estados Unidos Mexicanos, Que Reforma la del 5 de Febrero de 1857).[16] The 1917 Constitution adopted from the 1857 Constitution the chapters on territorial organization, civil liberties, democratic forms, anti-clerical clauses, and anti-monopolies clauses.

Although the 1857 Constitution served as a foundation for the 1917 Constitution, there are major, fundamental differences between them. They differ basically in approach. Both constitutions define and articulate democratic political rights and duties, but the 1917 Constitution goes on to include economic, social, and cultural rights.[17] The inclusion of these rights in the 1917 Constitution was original and revolutionary at the time.[18] A leading Mexican legal scholar has stated that, "the importance of the Mexican Constitution of 1917 is the systematic establishment of basic rights of economic and social integration."[19]

Another fundamental difference between the 1857 Constitution and the 1917 Constitution is in the different philosophical approaches to governing the nation that the different constitutions embrace. The 1857 Constitution called for a politically neutral federal government, a federal government that would be passive in relation to economic and social matters, a federal government that respects the status quo.[20] The 1917 Constitution on the other hand calls for a federal government that has a moral obligation to take an active role in promoting the social, economic, and cultural well-being of the people.[21]

The Federal Constitution is the most important political document in Mexico. It is the source and origin for all Mexican law. The hierarchy of sources of law in the civil law tradition to which Mexico's legal system belongs are, "constitution, legislation, regulation, and custom."[22] The constitution is the supreme law of the land, legislation is second only to the constitution, and regulation will override all custom.

The 1917 Mexican Constitution calls for a "federal, democratic, representative Republic composed of free and sovereign States."[23] All public power is derived from the people.[24] The country, whose official name is the United Mexican States (Estados Unidos Mexicanos), consists of 31 states and a Federal District.[25] Mexico City, the national capital, is located in the Federal District. There is a centralized federal goverment and individual state governments.[26] The federal government governs the Federal Distict.[27]

There are two articles in the 1917 Constitution that merit special mention because they are like no two articles in the U.S. Constitution. Articles 27 and 123 were adopted specifically to bring about the radical transformation of the nation and its people along lines defined by the 1917 Mexican Revolution.[28] Article 27 deals with agrarian reform and Article 123 deals with labor and social reform.

It is estimated that in 1910 almost ninety-seven percent of the arable land in Mexico was in the hands of no more that 1,000 families, while two percent belonged to small land holders, and one percent belonged to municipalities.[29] Article 27, which consists of over fifty paragraphs, was written with the intent of breaking up land, water, and other natural resource monopolies held by the privileged few.[30] The privilaged few not only consisted of the 1,000 Mexican Families mentioned previously, but also included the Church and foreign interests.

The first paragraph of Article 27 gives the nation original ownership "of the lands and waters within the boundaries of the national territory". Paragraph 1 also gives the nation "the right to transmit title thereof to private persons, thereby constituting private property." Article 27 goes on to grant the nation the power to expropriate private property by indemnification for reasons of public utility and "to ensure a more equitable distribution of public wealth." Paragraph 3 states that "the Nation shall at all times have the right to impose on private property such limitations as the public interest may demand." Paragraphs 4 and 5 give the nation direct ownership of all subsoil resources.

Property rights of foreign citizens and foreign corporations are covered by Section I of Article 27. In part, Section I states that foreigners must agree to submit themselves to Mexican law, "and bind themselves not to invoke the protection of their government in matters relating thereto" to be able to acquire property and mining concessions. In case of noncompliance by foreign citizens and foreign corporations, their property or mining concessions are forfeited to the nation. Foreign ownership of real property is further limited by the last sentence of Section I which states that "under no circumstances may foreigners acquire direct ownership of lands or waters within a zone of one hundred kilometers along the frontiers and of fifty kilometers along the shores of the country."

Article 27, Section II contains clauses restricting real property ownership by religious organizations. Religious organizations cannot "acquire, hold, or administer real property or mortages there of; such property held at present either directly or through an intermediary shall revert to the Nation." Not only did all churches become the property of the nation, but the federal government was empowered to "determine which of them may continue to be devoted to their present purposes." Furthermore, all "Bishopries, rectories, seminaries, asylums and schools, shall at once become the property of the Nation by inherent right." Also "all places of public worship" built in the future would become the property of the state. Section II of Article 27 also restricts the real property that private and public charitable institutions and commercial stock companies may acquire.

Constitutional Article 27 altered "the theory of the inviolability of private property" in the Mexican legal system.[31] The "economic interest" of the people and the nation were viewed as paramount when compared against the rights to private property by the framers of the 1917 Constitution. But Paragraph 1 of Article 14 of the 1917 Constitution seems to conflict with Article 27. This reaffirms the sanctity of private property in the constitution.

Article 123 consists of 31 paragraphs. The article was written with the intent of incorporating "extensive constitutional protections for labor."[32] It was also written "as a means of achieving" a just society.[33] This article places all labor matters under federal jurisdiction, though some limited authority is delegated to states in creating conciliation and arbitration boards.[34]

Article 123 covers three different aspects of benefit to workers. The first part concerns workers rights: an eight hour workday, a seven hour work night, special limits in the work of minors and women, maternity leave, mandatory vacation, mandatory days of rest, a safe working place, job security, minimum wage, overtime pay, and comparable pay. The second part of the Article deals with workers' compensation. Workers are entitled to compensation by their employers for injuries, death, or occupational diseases incurred as a result of their employment. There is no requirement to show fault or negligence" and contributory negligence is no defense."[35] The recoverable amount, which tends to be very low when compared to our workmen compensation in the United States, is set by law.[36] The third part concerns labor management relations. Workers are given the right to organize and bargain collectively. Workers also have the right to strike, with few reservations.[37] Workers are entitled to profit sharing, and the percentage of profits workers are entitled to are set by a national committee.[38] Finally, workers cannot be fired except for certain causes set out in statutes.[39]

Another article of the 1917 Constitution that is important is Article 49, which established the organization and division of the powers of the federal government. The federal government is divided into executive, legislative, and judicial branches. Each branch is independent of the other and "two or more of the powers shall never be united in one single person or corporation."[40] The executive is empowered to assume sole control of the government in case of emergencies. The emergencies and procedures for the executive to assume sole control of the government are defined and articulated in Article 29.

The executive branch is the branch of government in Mexico with the most political power. The office of the presidency is "the most important political and constitutional office" in Mexico.[41] The president, elected to a 6-year term with no reelection, has attained a position of supreme power through "long standing practice, statutory, and constitutional provisions, and a well-institutionalized tradition of near absolute political power."[42] The constitutional powers of the president include "broad power of appointment and removal, fiscal powers, the power to initiate and veto legislation, and control of the military."[43] Articles 81 through 93 of the 1917 Constitution delineate the president's powers and reponsibilities.

The legislative branch of the federal government is composed of the Senate and the Chamber of Deputies. There are two senators per state and one deputy for every 250,000

people in a state. Senators are elected by
direct popular vote to a six-year term.
Deputies are elected to a three-year term.
Three-fourths of the deputies are elected by
direct popular vote, with the remaining one-
fourth selected in proportion to the votes
received by each political party. Senators and
deputies cannot be reelected for an
immediately succeeding term.

Regular legislative sessions begin on
September 1 and must end by December 31 of
each year, although a special session may be
called. The special session must be called by
the Permanent Committee. The Permanent
Committee is composed of fifteen deputies and
fourteen senators. The members of the
Permanent Committee are elected by their
respective chambers at the end of each regular
legislative session.[44] During adjournment, the
Permanent Committee remains to handle
housekeeping chores.

The Mexican Constitution empowers both
the executive and the legislative branches to
initiate legislation, but only the Chamber of
Deputies can initiate bills concerning loans,
taxes, imposts, and the recruitment of troops.
However, in practice the executive branch
initiates almost all legislation and certainly
all legislation of any consequence.[45] Each new
bill must pass both Chambers by a majority
vote. The president has the power of the veto,
which the legislative branch can override by
a two-thirds vote in each Chamber. Once a
piece of legislation is passed by the Senate
and Chamber of Deputies, the bill is sent to
the president for promulgation of the bill.
Promulgation consists of the president
"recognizing the authenticity and regularity
of the legislation."[46] The president then has
the new law published in the official
government newspaper (Diario de la
Federacion). The president also issues the

"reglamento" for the new law--the rules and
regulations that give effect to the more
general provisions of the new law. The
"reglamento" has the same force as the new law
to which it refers.[47]

The federal judiciary in Mexico is based
on a three-tier system similar to our own
federal judiciary.[48] There is a Supreme Court
(Suprema Corte de Justicia de la Nacion),
which has final appellate jurisdiction over
all state and federal courts. There are
circuit courts (Tribunales de Circuito), which
are the federal appellate courts. The circuit
courts are divided into single judge courts
(Tribunales Unitarios de Circuito) and
collegiate courts (Tribunales Colegiados de
Circuito). There are also district courts
(Juzgados de Distrito) and jury courts
(Jurados Populares Federales), which are the
federal courts of first instance.[49]

The Supreme Court is composed of twenty
Justices and one Chief Justice. There are also
five Supernumerary Justices (Ministros
Supernumerarios). The Supernumerary Justices
serve as substitute justices when a Supreme
Court justice is temporarily unable to attend
a session.[50] Supreme Court justices are
appointed with life tenure by the president
with the approval of the Senate.[51] The
president also has the power to remove a
Supreme Court justice with the approval of the
Senate and the Chamber of Deputies.[52] The
Supreme Court meets in plenary session for
cases involving jurisdictional issues,
constitutional issues, and agrarian issues.[53]
The Supreme Court also divides and meets in
panels (salas). There are four panels:
criminal panel, civil panel, administrative
panel, and labor panel.

Circuit judges and district judges are appointed by the Supreme Court to four-year terms.[54] Circuit judges and district judges may be reappointed or promoted to a higher position at the end of the four-year term, but they may only be dismissed for bad conduct.[55]

The Constitution gives federal courts jurisdiction over controversies that arise out of laws or acts of state or federal authorities that violate individual guaranties, controversies between states or a state and federal authorities, all matters involving federal laws and treaties, all cases in which the federal government is a party, all matters involving maritime law, and all cases that involve members of the Diplomatic and Consular Corps.[56] The federal judiciary, vis-a-vis state judiciaries, " have a much larger share of the judicial power", in Mexico.[57]

One of the most important type of cases the federal courts hear in Mexico are "amparo" suits (juicio de amparo).[58] The "amparo" suit is an original Mexican institution with no exact equivalent in the common law tradition.[59] The word "amparo" literally means favor, aid, protection, or shelter. Legally the word encompasses elements of several legal actions of the common law tradition: writ of habeas corpus, injunction, error, mandamus, and certiorari.[60] There are five types of "amparo" suits: 1) "amparo" as a defense of individual rights such as life, liberty, and personal dignity; 2) "amparo" against laws (defending the individual against unconstitutional laws); 3) "amparo" in judicial matters (examine the legality of judicial decisions); 4) administrative "amparo" (providing jurisdiction against administrative enactments affecting the individual); and 5) "amparo" in agrarian matters (protecting the communal ejidal rights of the peasants).[61] The "amparo" suit may be either direct, initiated in the Supreme Court or collegiate circuit courts, or indirect, initiated in a district court and brought on appeal to the previously mentioned courts.

There are several federal judicial bodies in Mexico that are not part of the regular federal court structure. The most important are the Tax Court (Tribunal Fiscal de la Federacion), Labor Courts (Juntas de Conciliacion y Arbitraje), and Military Courts (Tribunales Militares). The Tax Court is an administrative court "with jurisdiction over controversies arising in fiscal matters between an individual and the government."[62] The Tax Court's responsibilities and structure are covered by the Fiscal Code (Codigo Fiscal de la Federacion) and the Organic Law of the Tax Court (Ley Organica del Tribunal Fiscal de la Federacion). The Labor Courts have jurisdiction over claims by workers that allege that their rights under the Federal Labor Code have been violated, disputes over collective bargaining, and strike-related matters.[63] Labor courts' responsibilities and structure are covered by the Federal Labor Law (Ley Federal del Trabajo). The Military Courts deal with military matters.[64] The Military Courts' responsibilities and structure are covered by the Organic Law of the Military Courts (Ley Organica de los Tribunales Militares).

Mexico's legal system stems from the civil law tradition. This occurred as a result of Mexico's long association with Spain. It is important to be aware of some of the most important concepts of the civil law tradition in order to formulate research strategies in conducting research into Mexican law. The civil law tradition is the oldest and most widely used legal tradition in the world today.[65] Its foundations were developed in the

Italian universities of the Renaissance when Roman law was rediscovered. Modern-day civil law is based on roman law (Corpus Juris Civilis), canon law (Roman Catholic Church), medieval common commercial law, secular natural law, secular positive law, and to a lesser degree custom law. The civil law tradition divides the law into two major areas of law: private law and public law. Private law concerns the legal relationships between individuals. Public law concerns the legal relationships between individuals and the state.

The most important contributions of roman law, canon law, and medieval commercial law to the civil law tradition are found in the private law area. Roman law influenced "the law of persons, the family, inheritance, property, torts, unjust enrichment, and contracts."[66] The influence of canon law is found mainly "in the area of family law and succession (both parts of the Roman Civil Law), criminal law and the law of procedures."[67] The third historical component, medieval common commercial law, is most evident in the commercial codes of the modern civil law tradition.[68] The most important contributions of secular natural law and secular positive law are in the public law area . They are most evident in constitution law, administrative law, and the judiciary.[69] The main tenets of the civil law tradition concern areas dealing with persons, things and obligations, and their relationship.[70] These legal tenets are found and expressed in the most important codes of the modern civil law states: the civil code, the commercial code, the criminal code, the code of civil procedures, and the code of criminal procedures.[71]

Codes in the civil law tradition have been written through the years on the assumption that by using a rational scholarly process, rules and laws can be formulated to apply to most all situations that may arise. As a result, codes tend to be very detailed and vast in size. The Mexican codes, like most Latin American codes, borrowed greatly from the European codes of the late nineteenth century.[72] Individual articles in the codes are not regarded as narrow rules. If no applicable article is found for a given situation, several articles may be viewed in combination, and a general rule may be deduced from the articles to reach a solution. Ideally, the code article or articles that are relevant are found and applied in an almost mechanical fashion to the given situation with no need for any legal interpretation. Of course, in practice in our modern complex world, all situations of possible legal conflict cannot be foreseen and provided for. Many situations occur where legal interpretation is required. In these situations the fact that the civil law tradition had its origins in the universities and not in the courts is significant. The civil law tradition was developed by legal scholars and not by judges and lawyers, as is the case with the common law tradition. Thus, the "authorities" of the civil law tradition were, and continue to be, legal scholars and not judges and lawyers.

The legal scholars of the civil law tradition produce legal treaties that are referred to as doctrine ("doctrina" in Mexico). Civil law tradition judges, lawyers, and law students will refer to the doctrine of the leading legal scholars as common law tradition judges, lawyers, and law students will refer to case law. According to John H. Merryman, "the law in a civil jurisdiction is what the scholars say it is."[73]

The legal principle of "stare decisis," of the common law tradition is not recognized in the civil law tradition. There are several reasons for the rejection of the legal principle of "stare decisis" by the civil law tradition. One reason is the fact that the civil law tradition was developed by legal scholars in the universities and not by judges in the courtroom. Another reason is the post-French Revolutionary influence on the civil law tradition. The post-French Revolution legislature sought to reform the judiciary to prevent previous abuses.[74] The role of the judge was reduced "to that of a minor bureaucrat who had no power to go beyond the letter of the law."[75] Judicial review of legislation was not within the legal powers of judges.[76] No one but the elected legislature had the power to create law.

Although the principle of "stare decisis" is not recognized in the civil law tradition, the Mexican judiciary does create case law to some extent.[77] The Supreme Court and federal collegiate courts may establish a formally binding precedent called "jurisprudencia."[78] "Jurisprudencia" is established by having five consecutive and consistent decisions on a point of law. "Jurisprudencia" is binding on the court that established it and on all lower federal and state courts. Many of the legal treatises listed in the guide have the word "jurisprudencia" in their title. It is important to remember that in these instances "jurisprudencia" means case law and not the general study of law.

The starting point for nearly all Mexican legal research is a code. But, before going into the Mexican codes, it is important to mention some introductory material on the Mexican legal system. The most complete introduction is An Introduction to the Mexican Legal System by James E. Herget and Jorge

Camil (1978). A reprint of this work appears in volume I of <u>Modern Legal Systems Cyclopedia</u>, edited by Kenneth Robert Redden (1984-). <u>Compendium of the Laws of Mexico</u> (1938) is dated but is still useful to someone unfamiliar with the Mexican legal system.

Although they are not true introductions to the legal system of Mexico, the following sources also should be considered: <u>An Introduction to the History of Mexican Law</u> by Guillermo Floris Margadant (1983); <u>Foreign Law: Current Sources of Codes and Legislation in Jurisdictions of the World</u> by Thomas H. Reynolds and Arturo A. Fores (1989-); <u>A Revised Guide to the Law and Legal Literature of Mexico</u> by Helen L. Clagett and David M. Valderrama (1973); and <u>Guide to the Law and Legal Literature of Mexican States</u> (1979) by Helen L. Clagett, a reprint of a 1947 edition.

As mentioned before, the starting point for nearly all Mexican legal research is a code. The first step in the process is to determine which code is the relevant one. Forty-one subject headings and an index have been provided to facilitate this process. The subject headings are based on broad general legal terms. For an example, under "Domestic Relations" all laws associated with family law are included: marriage laws, divorce laws, adoption laws, legal guardianship laws, emancipation of minors laws, paternity and filiation laws, homestead laws, and civil registry laws.

Once the relevant code is determined, the specific code article or articles that apply to the specific situation must be located. Keyword searching, as used in most legal research, is not applicable in Mexican legal research. Mexican codes do not have indexes; instead, codes provide a short, general table of contents. The table of contents can be located either at the front of the code or at the back of the code. In Mexican legal research, the search is done by thinking in broad, general legal concepts and then working down to the specific. As an example, the search in the Mexican civil code for the divorce articles would not start with "divorce" but with "of persons" since divorce deals with a relationship of persons. Under the "of persons" heading one would find divorce, marriage, adoptions, birth registration, death registration, and other matters relating to a person as a legal entity. A person becomes a legal entity at birth and loses this capacity at death.

Codes in Mexico are issued by private publishers. Two Mexican publishers dominate the code publishing trade. They are "Ediciones Andrade" and "Editorial Porrua." "Ediciones Andrade" publishes the majority of the codes in a loose-leaf format, with regular updating. The other codes are published in a paperback format. Besides the loose-leaf updating service, "Ediciones Andrade" offers other good features. One feature is the practice of not only including the specific code but of including all of the legislation and regulations relevant to the specific code. A third good feature of "Ediciones Andrade" codes is that they are annotated.

"Editorial Porrua" publishes the codes in a paperback format. They issue new editions continuously, and these editions are more like reprints rather than new editions. "Editorial Porrua" also adds relevant legislation and regulations to the codes as "Ediciones Andrade" does, but not to the extent that "Ediciones Andrade" does. The good features of "Editorial Porrua" are that the codes are extremely inexpensive (about $10.50), and there is no loose-leaf filing requirement. The codes can be replaced on a yearly basis, which

assures that the material is current.
"Editorial Porrua" codes are not annotated.
"Editorial Porrua" publishes two series that
include most all codes and major regulations.
The first series, "Leyes y Codigos de Mexico,"
features federal legislation. The second
series, "Codigos de los Estados de la
Republica Mexicana" features state legislation
from the various Mexican states. A third
series, "Biblioteca Juridica Porrua," is
composed of doctrinal treatises by the most
prominent legal scholars of Mexico.

Several of the major codes of Mexico in
the civil and commercial area have been
translated into English. Michael Wallace
Gordon has translated the Mexican Civil Code.
The Foreign Tax Association has translated the
Mexican Commercial Code, the Social Security
Code, the Tax Code, the Labor Code, and the
regulations concerning foreign investment in
Mexico. The Foreign Tax Association's
translations of the codes are in loose-leaf
format and thus always up-to-date. Matthew
Bender's three-volume Doing Business in Mexico
also provides English translations of business
oriented legislation and regulations in a
loose-leaf format. The other major codes of
the Mexican legal system, the Criminal Code,
the Civil Procedures Code, and the Criminal
Procedures Code, have not been translated into
English.

The second step in Mexican legal research
involves finding the doctrine that applies to
the situation under study. Most of the
doctrine is organized by code and articles
chronologically, which makes for easy access.
As is the case with codes, the doctrinal
treatises do not have indexes with few
exceptions, but provide only a short, general
table of contents. "Editorial Porrua"
publishes the works of the more renowned
Mexican legal scholars in the previously

mentioned series, "Biblioteca Juridica Porrua." The "Instituto de Investigaciones Juridicas" (Institute for Legal Studies) of the Law School at the National Autonomous University of Mexico is another source of doctrinal treatises. The "Instituto de Investigaciones Juridicas" in conjunction with "Editorial Porrua" also publish excellent doctrinal treatises. Several sources of doctrine are listed under each of the subject headings in the body of this work.

The Index to Foreign Legal Periodicals indexes three major Mexican law reviews which are an excellent source for doctrine. The Mexican Law Reviews are "Revista de la Faculta de Derecho de Mexico," "Boletin Mexicano de Derecho Comparado," and "Revista de Investigaciones Juridicas." These law reviews may be purchased directly from the Law School of the National Autonomous University of Mexico, or through the Faxon Company.

All of the doctrine sources previously mentioned are in Spanish. English-language secondary material, which is not doctrine, can be found by using INFOTRACT, Current Law Index, and Index to Legal Periodicals. Several sources for secondary material in English are listed under each of the subject headings used in this work, as well as Spanish-language doctrinal sources.

The third step in Mexican legal research is the most difficult one. This step involves searching for Supreme Court "jurisprudencia" and "tesis sobresalientes." "Tesis sobresalientes" are case decisions of note that have persuasive value, but are not binding on lower courts as is the case with "jurisprudencia." Decisions of the Supreme Court are officially published in the "Semanrio Judicial de la Federacion" (Judicial Weekly of the Federation).[79] The "Semanario" is

broken down into series called "Epocas." There
have been seven "Epocas": First "Epoca," 1871-
1874, Second "Epoca," 1881-1889, Third
"Epoca," 1890-1897, Fourth "Epoca," 1898-
1910, Fifth "Epoca," 1918-1957, Sixth "Epoca,"
1957-1968, and Seventh "Epoca," 1969-.

The first four "Epocas" (1871-1910) are
called "jurisprudencia historica" (historical
jurisprudence). "Jurisprudencia historica" has
no binding force and is used only for
historical legal studies.[80] The reason that
"jurispudencia historica" has no binding force
is that the current Mexican Constitution was
not adopted until 1917, and anything not based
on the 1917 Constitution has no legal force.
The "jurisprudencia aplicable" (applicable
jurisprudence) starts with the fifth "Epoca"
in 1918.[81]

Access to the Supreme Court decisions in
the "Semanario" is extremely difficult and
time consuming. The reason for this is the
constantly changing manner of indexing and
terms used for topic access. They not only
change from "Epoca" to "Epoca," but even from
volume to volume from within the same "Epoca."
The changes are too many to allow for a
discussion in this introduction. Ezequiel
Guerrero Lara's work, cited in footnote 79, is
the one source on how to use the "Semanario."

The difficulty of accessing Supreme Court
decisions in the "Semanario" has led to
private publishers publishing Supreme Court
decisions in more accessible formats. "Mayo
Ediciones" offers the better and most complete
reporting service. "Mayo Ediciones" published
"Jurisprudencia y Tesis Sobresalientes"
(Jurisprudence and Cases of Note), which
brings together case decisions that are
binding and case decisions that have
persuasive value. The decisions are arranged
by Supreme Court panel (criminal, civil,

administrative, labor, and plenary session). Within each group the decisions are arranged by topic. This title by itself will suffice in most cases for all Supreme Court decisions' research.

"Mayo Ediciones" also publishes "Jurisprudencia; Poder Judicial de la Federacion" (Jurisprudence; Judicial Power of the Federation) which does not include cases of note, only "jurisprudencia." Another publication of "Ediciones Mayo" is "Informe" (Report) which is the annual report of the Supreme Court. The most important cases of the year are reported in the "Informe". A third publication of "Mayo Ediciones" is "Compilacion Mayo del Semanario Judicial de la Federacion" (Mayo Compilation of the Judicial Weekly of the Federation). The compilation arranges the decisions by Supreme Court panel, and by topic within each panel.

Another important source for "jurisprudencia" are treatises that bring together "jurisprudencia" relating to the Constitution and the various legal codes. I have listed this type of treatise under the Subject Heading to which it relates. Under the subject heading of "Miscellaneous," subheading "Jurisprudence and the Supreme Court" are listed other general sources for "jurisprudencia." One final word on "jurisprudencia;" published case decisions are condensed to a point that most common law researchers would consider extreme. Seldom is there a statement of facts included in the reported decisions. What tends to be published is the "considerando" (conclusion of law) or the thesis of the case with only those facts of the case needed to make the published ruling comprehensible.

The three steps in Mexican legal research are: finding the relevant article or articles in the appropriate code, finding the relevant "doctrina," and finding the relevant "jurisprudencia." The most important step is the first. The research process could stop at this step if the researcher felt confident enough to assume that the correct article or articles had been found and their correct interpretation achieved. However, my own experience is that the majority of people who work with Mexican law do not stop after the first step; rather they go on to step two. Finding the appropriate "doctrina" is really essential to good Mexican legal research. Step three seems to vary in importance according to the researcher's legal background. Mexican-trained lawyers do not consider step three essential; American-trained lawyers do believe that step three is essential. Mexican lawyers are trained in the civil law tradition, and American lawyers are trained in the common law tradition. But also important is the fact that "jurisprudencia" research is so difficult because of the lack of finding tools. More and more finding tools are being published in Mexico to provide easier access to "jurisprudencia." The importance of step three will thus increase as more and more finding tools are published in Mexico.

Administrative Laws

PRIMARY MATERIAL

1. Ley de Adquisiciones, Arrendamientos y
    Prestacion de Servicios Relacionados con
    Bienes Muebles (2-8-85).
    Law of Acquisitions, Leasing and
    Services Related to Chattels (Related to
    Government Entities).

2. Ley de Imprenta (4-12-17).
    Publishing Law (Public Press).

3. Ley de Informacion Estadistica y
    Geografica (12-30-80).
    Statistical and Geographic Information
    Law.

4. Ley de Obras Publicas (12-30-80).
    Public Works Law.

5. Ley de Planeacion (1-5-83).
    National Planning Law (Master Plan for
    the Federal Government).

6. Ley del Diario Oficial de la Federacion
    y Gaceta Gubernamentales (12-24-86).
    Law of the Official Daily of the
    Federation and Government Gazettes.

7.   Ley del Presupuesto, Contabilidad y
     Gastos Publicos (12-31-76).
     Budget, Accounting and Public Expenses
     Law.

8.   Ley del Servicio Militar y Su Reglamento
     (9-11-40).
     Military Service Law and Its
     Regulations.

9.   Ley Federal de las Entitades
     Paraestatales (5-14-86).
     Federal Law of Parastate Institutions.

10. Ley Federal de Responsabilidades de los
     Servidores Publicos (12-31-82).
     Federal Civil Service Responsibility
     Law.

11. Ley Federal Sobre Monumentos y Zonas
     Arqueologicas, Artisticas e Historicas
     (5-6-72).
     Federal Law on Monuments and
     Archaeological, Artistic and Historical
     Zones.

12. Ley General de Bienes Nacionales
     (1-8-82).
     General Law of National Assets.

13. Ley General de Deuda Publica (12-31-76).
     General Law of the Public Debt.

14. Ley General de Poblacion (1-7-74).
     General Population Law.

15. Ley Organica de la Administracion
     Publica Federal (12-29-76).
     Organic Law of the Federal Public
     Administration.

16. Ley Organica de la Loteria Nacional para
     la Asistencia Public (1-14-85).
     Organic Law of the National Lottery for
     Public Assistance.

17. Ley para el Control, por Parte del
     Gobierno Federal, de los Organismos
     Descentralizados y Empresas de
     Participacion Estatal (12-31-70).
     Law for the Control, by the Federal
     Government, of the Decentralized
     Agencies and Companies in Partnership
     with the State.

18. Ley Sobre el Escudo, la Bandera y el
     Himno Nacional (2-8-84).
     National Shield, National Flag and
     National Anthem Law.

LOCATION OF LEGISLATION

19. Ley Organica de la Administracion
     Publica Federal. 24a ed. Mexico:
     Editorial Porrua, 1989.
     "Organic Law of the Federal Public
     Administration."

20. Constitucion Political Mexicana: Con
     Reformas y Adiciones al Dia. Mexico:
     Ediciones Andrade, 1967-. Loose-Leaf
     Service.
     "Mexican Political Constitution: With
     Reforms and Up-to-Date Additions."

SECONDARY MATERIAL: SERIALS

21. Acosta Romero, M. "Unilateralidad del
     Acto Administrativo en el Derecho
     Mexicano." Revista de la Facultad de
     Derecho de Mexico 29 (January-April
     1979): 11-38.
     "The One-Sidedness of the Administrative
     Act in Mexican Law."

22. Cortes, C. "Justicia Administrativa
     Reformada." Revista de la Facultad de
     Derecho de Mexico 28 (May-August 1978):
     385-398.
     "Reformed Administrative Justice."

23. Cortinas-Pelaez, L. "Teoria General de
     los Cometidos del Poder Publico."
     Revista de Administracion Publica 111
     (1986): 51-93.
     "General Theory of Government Power."

24. Diaz Rivera, E. I. "Las Casas de Bolsa
     en la Actividad Fiduciaria." Revista de
     la Faculdad de Derecho de Mexico 34
     (1984): 723-727.
     "The Stock-Exchange in Trust
     Activities."

25. Gonzalez-Cosio, A. "Poder Publico y la
     Jurisdiccion en Material Administrativa
     en Mexico." Revista de Administracion
     Publica 80 (May-August 1976): 439-509.
     "Government Power and Jurisdiction in
     Administrative Matters in Mexico."

26. Onecha Santamaria, C. "Estudio de
     Organizacion Administrativa." La
     Justicia 34 (October 1977): 9-16.
     "A Study of Administrative
     Organization."

27. Ovalle Favela, J. "Algunas
    Consideraciones Sobre la Justicia
    Administrativa en el Derecho Comparado y
    en el Ordenamiento Mexicano." Revista de
    la Facultad de Derecho de Mexico 28
    (May-August 1978): 441-471.
    "Some Thoughts on Administrative Justice
    in Comparative Law and Mexican Law."

28. Ruiz Massieu, M. "Notas Sobre el Cuerpo
    Consultivo Agrario." Boletin Mexicano de
    Derecho Comparado 13 (September-December
    1980): 787-806.
    "Notes on the Consultive Agrarian
    Board."

SECONDARY MATERIAL: MONOGRAPHS

29. Acosta Romero, Miguel, and Rafael I.
    Martinez Morales. Catalog de
    Ordenamiento Juridicos de la
    Administracion Publica Federal: Panorama
    de la Legislacion Aministrativa. 3a ed.
    Mexico: Editorial Porrua, 1989.
    "Catalog of Juridical Ordinances of the
    Federal Public Administration: Panorama
    of Administrative Legislation."

30. Acosta Romero, Miguel. Teoria General
    del Derecho Administrativo. 9a ed.
    Mexico: Editorial Porrua, 1990.
    "General Theory of Administrative Law."

31. Carrillo Flores, Antonio. La Justicia
    Federal y la Administracion Publica. 2a
    ed. Mexico: Editorial Porrua, 1973.
    "Federal Jurisdiction and the Public
    Administration."

32. Faya Viesca, Jacinto. Administracion Publica Federal: La Nueva Estructura. 2a ed. Mexico: Editorial Porrua, 1983. "Federal Public Administration: The New Structure."

33. Fraga, Gabino. Derecho Administrativo. 28a ed. Mexico: Editorial Porrua, 1989. "Administrative Law."

34. Garcia Dominguez, Miguel Angel. Las Multas Administrativas Federales y Su Impugnacion: Prontuatio de Disposiciones Juridicas. Mexico: UNAM, 1985. "Federal Administrative Fines and Their Refutation: A Memorandum Book of Juridical Provisions."

35. Gonzalez Cosio, Arturo. El Poder Publico y la Jurisdiccion en Material Administrativa en Mexico. 2a ed. Mexico: Editorial Porrua, 1982. "Government Power and Its Jurisdiction in Administrative Matters in Mexico."

36. Gonzalez Perez, Jesus. Derecho Procesal Administrativo Mexicano. Mexico: Editorial Porrua, 1988. "Mexican Administrative Procedure."

37. Perez de Leon E., Enrique. Notas de Derecho Constitucional y Administrativo. 10a ed. Mexico: Editorial Porrua, 1990. "Notes on Constitutional and Administrative Law."

38. Pina Vara, Rafael de. Diccionario de los Organos de la Administracion Publica Federal. Mexico: Editorial Porrua, 1983. "Dictionary of the Departments of the Federal Public Administration."

39. Secretaria de la Presidencia. Prontuario de Disposiciones Juridicas para las Secretarias y Departamentos de Estado. 3a ed. Mexico: Direccion de Estudios Administrativos. 1972.
"Memorandum Book of Juridical Provisions for Federal Agencies and Departments."

40. Rendon Huerta Barrera, Teresita. Derecho Municipal. Mexico: Editorial Porrua, 1985.
"Municipal Law."

41. Rios Elizondo, Roberto. El Acto de Gobierno: El Poder y el Derecho Administrativo. Mexico: Editorial Porrua, 1975.
"The Actions of the Government: The Authority and Administrative Law."

42. Ruiz Massieu, Jose Francisco. Estudios Juridicos Sobre la Nueva Administracion Publica Mexicana. Mexico: Editorial Limusa, 1981.
"Juridical Studies on the New Mexican Public Administration."

43. Serra Rojas, Andres. Derecho Administrativo: Doctrina, Legislacion y Jurisprudencia. 12a ed. Mexico: Editorial Porrua, 1988.
"Administrative Law: Doctrine, Legislation and Jurisprudence."

44. Tribunal Fiscal de la Federacion. Cuarenta y Cinco Anos al Servicio de Mexico. Mexico: El Tribunal, 1982.
"Tax Court of the Federation: Forty-Five Years at the Service of Mexico."

Agrarian Reform Laws

PRIMARY MATERIAL

45. Ley de Terrenos Baldios Nacionales y
    Demasias (2-7-51).
    Law of Undeveloped National Land and
    Excess Land.

46. Ley Federal de Reforma Agraria
    (4-16-71).
    Federal Agrarian Reform Law.

47. Ley General de Credito Rural (4-5-76).
    General Law of Rural Credit.

48. Ley Organica del Sistema BanRural
    (1-13-86).
    Organic Law of the "BanRural" System
    (Rural Bank).

49. Ley Reglamentaria del Parrafo 3 del
    Articulo 27 Constitucional (3-12-46).
    Regulatory Law of Paragraph 3 of Article
    27 of the Constitution.

LOCATION OF LEGISLATION

50. Codificacion Agraria y Leyes Sobre
    Tierras Con Reglamentos, Acuerdos y
    Disposiciones Complementarias. 8a ed.,
    Mexico: Ediciones Andrade, 1984. Loose-
    Leaf Service.
    "Argrarian Codification and Laws on Land
    with Regulations, Accords and
    Complementary Provisions."

51. Ley Federal de Reforma Agraria. 30a ed.,
    Mexico: Editorial Porrua, 1989.
    "Federal Agrarian Reform Law."

SECONDARY MATERIAL: SERIALS

52. "Mexican Agrarian Rights: Who Do They
    Benefit?" California Western Journal 8
    (Winter 1978): 130-170.

SECONDARY MATERIAL: MONOGRAPHS

53. Chavez Padron de Velazquez, Martha. El
    Derecho Agrario en Mexico. 9a ed.
    Mexico: Editorial Porrua, 1988.
    "Agrarian Law in Mexico."

54. Chavez Padron de Velazquez, Martha. El
    Proceso Social Agrario y Sus
    Procedimientos. 5a ed. Mexico: Editorial
    Porrua, 1986.
    "The Social Agrarian Process and Its
    Procedure."

55. Craig, Ann L. The First Agraristas: An
    Oral History of a Mexican Agrarian
    Reform Movement. Berkeley: University of
    California Press, 1983.

56. Gonzalez G., Tarsicio. Los Campesinos y la Reforma Agraria Integral. Mexico: Ediciones Oasis, 1970.
"The Farm Workers and the Integral Agrarian Reform."

57. Ibarrola, Antonio de. Derecho Agrario. 3a ed. Mexico: Editorial Porrua, 1948.
"Agrarian Law."

58. Lemus Garcia, Raul. Derecho Agrario Mexicano. 6a ed. Mexico: Editorial Porrua, 1987.
"Mexican Agrarian Law."

59. Luna Arroyo, Antonio. Derecho Agrario Mexicano: Antecedentes, Dogmatica y Critica. Mexico: Editorial Porrua, 1975.
"Mexican Agrarian Law: Antecedents, Dogmatic and Analysis."

60. Luna Arroyo, Antonio y Luis G. Alcerreca. Diccionario de Derecho Agrario Mexicano. Mexico: Editorial Porrua, 1982.
"Dictionary of Agrarian Law."

61. Manzanilla Schaffer, Victor. Reforma Agraria Mexicana. 2a ed. Mexico: Editorial Porrua, 1986.
"Mexican Agrarian Reform."

62. Mendieta y Nunez, Lucio. El Problema Agrario de Mexico y la Ley Federal de Reforma Agraria. 18a ed. Mexico: Editorial Porrua, 1982.
"The Agrarian Problem of Mexico and the Federal Law of Agrarian Reform."

63. Mendieta y Nunez, Lucio. <u>El Sistema Agrario Constitucional</u>. 5a ed. Mexico: Editorial Porrua, 1980.
"The Agrarian System and the Constitution."

64. Reyes Osorio, Sergio. <u>Reforma Agraria: Tres Ensayos</u>. Mexico: Ediciones Productividad, 1969.
"Agrarian Reform: Three Essays."

65. Romero Espinosa, Emilio. <u>La Reforma Agraria en Mexico, A Medio Siglo de Iniciada</u>. Mexico: Cuadernos Americanos, 1963.
"The Agrarian Reform in Mexico, Half a Century After Its Beginning."

66. Sanderson, Susan Walsh. <u>Land Reform in Mexico, 1910-1980</u>. Orlando: Academic Press, 1984.

67. Silva Herzog, Jesus. <u>El Agrarismo Mexicano y la Reforma Agraria: Exposicion y Critica</u>. 2a ed. Mexico: Fondo de Cultura Economica, 1964.
"Mexican Agrarianism and the Agrarian Reform; Exposition and Examination."

Aliens and Nationality Laws

PRIMARY LAWS

68. Ley de Impuestos de Migracion (12-31-
    73).
    Immigration Tax Law.

69. Ley de Nacionalidad y Naturalizacion
    (1-20-34).
    Nationality and Naturalization Law.

70. Ley General de Poblacion (1-7-74).
    General Population Law.

71. Ley Organica de la Fraccion 1 del
    Articulo 27 de la Constitucion General
    (1-21-26).
    Organic Law of Section 1 of Article 27
    of the General Constitution.

LOCATION OF LEGISLATION

72. Extranjeria, Turismo y Poblacion:
    Contiene Ademas Ley Federal de
    Estadisticas y su Reglamento Asi Como
    Disposiciones Conexas. Mexico: Ediciones
    Andrade, 1962-. Loose-Leaf Service.

"Alienage, Tourism and Population: Also Contains the Federal Law of Statistics and Its Regulations as Well as Related Legislation."

73. See below, entries 75 and 77.

SECONDARY MATERIAL: SERIALS

74. Ziskind, David and Esther Horney. "Laws Affecting Migratory Labor: United States, Mexico, and Canada." <u>Comparative Labor Law</u> 4 (Winter 1981): 1-25.

SECONDARY MATERIAL: MONOGRAPHS

75. Bravo Caro, Rodolfo. <u>Guia del Extranjero</u>. 12a ed. Mexico: Editorial Porrua, 1988.
"Guide for the Foreigner."

76. Dunn, Frederick Sherwood. <u>The Diplomatic Protection of Americans in Mexico</u>. New York: Kraus Reprint, 1972.

77. Echanove Trujillo, Carlos A. <u>Manual del Extranjero</u>. 19a ed. Mexico: Editorial Porrua, 1976.
"Handbook for the Foreigner."

78. Pina, Rafael de. <u>Estatuto Legal de los Extranjeros: Texto al Dia, Notas y Jurisprudencia</u>. 3a ed. Mexico: Ediciones Botas, 1966.
"Legal Statutes Concerning Foreigners: Up-To-Date Text, Notes and Jurisprudence."

Amparo Laws

PRIMARY MATERIAL

79. Ley de Amparo Reglamentaria de los
     Articulos 103 y 107 de la Constitucion
     Politica de los Estados Unidos Mexicanos
     (1-10-36).
     "Amparo" Law Which Regulates Articles
     103 and 107 of the Political
     Constitution of the United Mexican
     States.

LOCATION OF LEGISLATION

80. <u>Nueva Legislacion de Amparo Reformada:
     Doctrina, Textos y Jurisprudencia,
     Codigo Federal de Procedimientos
     Civiles, Ley Organica del Poder Judicial
     Federal, y Sus Reformas</u>. Alberto Trueba
     Urbina y Jorge Trueba Barrera. 52a ed.
     Mexico: Editorial Porrua, 1990.
     "New Legislation of the Reformed Writ of
     'Amparo': Doctrine, Texts and
     Jurisprudence, Federal Code of Civil
     Procedure, Organic Law of the Federal
     Judiciary and Its Reforms."

81. *Constitucion Politica Mexicana: Con
     Reformas y Adiciones al Dia*. Mexico:
     Ediciones Andrade, 1935-. Loose-Leaf
     Service.
     "Mexican Political Constitution: With
     Reforms and Up-To-Date Additions."

SECONDARY MATERIAL: SERIALS

82. Arellano Garcia, C. "La Formula Otero y
     Amparo Contra Leyes." *Revista de
     Investigaciones Juridicas* 11 (1987):
     113-129.
     "The Otero Formula and the Writ of
     'Amparo' Against Laws."

83. Barajas Montes de Oca, S. "Lineamientos
     Generales del Amparo en Materia de
     Trabajo." *Boletin Mexicano de Derecho
     Comparado* 20 (1987): 447-487.
     "General Features of the Writ of
     'Amparo' in Labor Matters."

84. Cardenas, Raul F. "Arrest and Detention
     in Mexico." *International Commission of
     Jurist Review* (June 1984): 58-62.

85. Castro, J.V. "La Acta Competencia de la
     Suprema Corte de Justicia en Materia de
     Amparo." *Revista de Investigaciones
     Juridicas* 11 (1987): 165-170.
     "The Record of the Supreme Court of
     Justice in 'Amparo' Matters."

86. Castro, J.V. "Todavia Mas Sobre la
     Formula Otero." *Revista de
     Investigaciones Juridicas* 12 (1987): 65-
     77.
     "Still More on the Otero Formula."

87. Fix Zamudio, H.F. "Brief Introduction to the Mexican Writ of 'Amparo'." <u>California Western International Law Journal</u> 9 (Spring 1979): 306-348.

88. "Mexican Law Symposium. The Claim of 'Amparo' in Mexico: Constitutional Protection of Human Rights. P.P. Camargo; The Mexican Norariate. G.F. Margadant; Certain Aspects of Mexican Labor Laws, Especially as They Affect Foreign Owned Business. R.C. Villareal; Administrative Procedures Necessary to Secure a Patent in Mexico. Soni; Private International Law in Mexico and the United States: A Brief Comparative Study. J.L. Siqueiros." <u>California Western Law Review</u> 6 (Spring 1970): 201-266.

89. Rio Rodriguez, Carlos del. "Judicial Review Seen From a Mexican Perspective." <u>California Western International Law Journal</u> 20 (Winter 1989): 7-19.

90. Schwartz, C.E. "Exceptions to the Exhaustion of Administrative Remedies Under the Mexican Writ of 'Amparo': Some Possible Applications to Judicial Review in the United States." <u>California Western Law Review</u> 7 (Spring 1971): 331-353.

91. Soberanes Fernandez, J.L. "Algo Sobre los Antecedentes de Nuestro Juicio de Amparo." <u>Boletin Mexicano de Derecho Comparado</u> 21 (1988): 1067-1087. "Some thoughts on the Antecedents of Our Writ of 'Amparo'."

92. Tamayo y Salmoran, R. "El Poder y la Judicatura: Breve Comentario Sobre la jurisdiccion de Amparo y la Fusion Judicial." Boletin Mexicano de Derecho Comparado 21 (1988): 1089-1104. "Power and Judicature: A Brief Commentary on the Jurisdiction of `Amparo' and Judicial Merger."

SECONDARY MATERIAL: MONOGRAPHS

93. Acosta Romero, Miguel y Genaro David Gongora Pimentel. Ley de Amparo: Legislacion, Jurisprudencia, Doctrina. 2a ed. Mexico: Editorial Porrua, 1985. "The Law of `Amparo': Legislation, Jurisprudence, Doctrine."

94. Arellano Garcia, Carlos. El Juicio de Amparo. 2a ed. Mexico: Editorial Porrua, 1983. "The Writ of `Amparo'."

95. Baker, Richard D. Judicial Review in Mexico: A Study of the "Amparo" Suit. Austin: University of Texas, 1971.

96. Briseno Sierra, Humberto. Teoria y Tecnica del Amparo. Mexico: Editorial Porrua, 1966. "Theory and Technique of the Writ of `Amparo'."

97. Burgoa, Ignacio. Diccionario de Derecho Constitucional, Garantias y Amparo. Mexico: Editorial Porrua, 1982. "Dictionary of Constitutional Law, Guarantees and the Writ of `Amparo'".

98. Burgoa, Ignacio. El Juicio de Amparo. 27a ed. Mexico: Editorial Porrua, 1990. "The `Amparo' Suit."

99. Castro, Juventino V. <u>Garantias y Amparo</u>.
5a ed. Mexico: Editorial Porrua, 1986.
"Guaranties and the Writ of `Amparo'."

100. Castro, Juventino V. <u>Hacia el Amparo</u>
<u>Evolucionado</u>. 3a ed. Mexico: Editorial
Porrua, 1986.
"Towards the Evolving Writ of `Amparo'."

101. Castro Zavaleta, Salvador. <u>Practica del</u>
<u>Jucio de Amparo: Doctrina, Formularios y</u>
<u>Jurisprudencia</u>. 4a ed. Mexico: Cardenas,
1982.
"The `Amparo' Suit: Doctrine,
Formularies and Jurisprudence."

102. Estrella Mendez, Sebastian. <u>Estudio de</u>
<u>los Medios de Impugnacion en el Codigo</u>
<u>de Procedimientos Civiles para el</u>
<u>Distrito Federal y la Procedencia del</u>
<u>Juicio de Amparo</u>. 2a ed. Mexico:
Editorial Porrua, 1987.
"Study of the Means of Refutation in the
Civil Code for the Federal District and
Procedure for the Writ of `Amparo'."

103. Gongora Pimentel, Genaro. <u>Introduccion</u>
<u>al Estudio del Juicio de Amparo: El</u>
<u>Articulo 103 de la Constitucion Politica</u>
<u>de los Estados Unidos Mexicanos</u>. Mexico:
Editorial Porrua, 1987.
"Introduction to the Study of the Writ
of `Amparo': Article 103 of the
Political Constitution of the United
Mexican States."

104. Gonzalez Cosio, Arturo. <u>El Juicio de</u>
<u>Amparo</u>. 2a ed. Mexico: Editorial Porrua,
1985.
"The `Amparo' Suit."

105. Gonzalez Cosio, Arturo. El Poder Publico
     y la Jurisprudencia en Materia
     Administrativa en Mexico. 2a ed. Mexico:
     Editorial Porrua, 1982.
     "Government Power and Its Jurisdiction
     in Administrative Matters in Mexico."

106. Palacios, J. Ramon. Instituciones de
     Amparo. 2a ed. Mexico: Editorial Jose M.
     Cajica Jr., 1969.
     "Proceedings in the Writ of 'Amparo'."

107. Rabasa, Emilio. El Articulo 14, Estudio
     Constitucional, y el Juicio
     Constitucional: Origenes, Teoria y
     Extension. 4a ed. Mexico: Editorial
     Porrua, 1978.
     "Article 14, Constitutional Study, and
     Constitutional Jurisdiction: Origin,
     Theory and Scope."

108. Rosales Aguilar, Romulo. Formulario del
     Juicio de Amparo: Puesto al Dia con las
     Reformas a la Ley de Amparo, y con
     Apendice de Jurisprudencia Definida en
     Materia del Procedimiento del Juicio de
     Amparo. 6a ed. Mexico: Editorial Porrua,
     1990.
     "Writ of 'Amparo' Formulary: With Up-
     To-Date Reforms to the Law of 'Amparo',
     and with an Appendix of Jurisprudence on
     the Procedures of the Writ of 'Amapro'."

109. Sanchez Martinez, Francisco. Formulario
     del Juicio de Amparo y Jurisprudencia.
     5a ed. Mexico: Editorial Porrua, 1986.
     "Formulary of the Writ of 'Amparo' and
     Jurisprudence."

110. Trueba Urbina, Alberto y Jorge Trueba
     Barrera. Nueva Legislacion de Amparo
     Reformada: Doctrina, Textos, y
     Jurisprudencia. 49a ed. Mexico:

Editorial Porrua, 1988.
"New Reformed Legislation on the Writ of
'Amparo': Doctrine, Text and
Jurisprudence."

111. Vallarta, Ignacio Luis. El juicio de
Amparo y el Writ of Habeas Corpus.
Ensayo Critico-Comparativo Sobre Esos
Recursos Constitutcionales. Mexico:
Imprenta de J.J. Terrazas, 1896.
"The Writ of 'Amparo' and the Writ of
Habeas Corpus. A Critical-Comparative
Essay on These Constitutional Remedies."

Anti-Trust Laws

PRIMARY MATERIAL

112. Ley Organica del Articulo 28
     Constitucional en Materia de Monopolias
     (8-31-34)(12-27-74).
     Organic Law of Article 28 of the
     Constitution in Matters Relating to
     Monopolies.

LOCATION OF LEGISLATION

113. Constitucion Politica Mexicana: Con
     Reformas y Adiciones al Dia. Mexico:
     Ediciones Andrade, 1935-. Loose Leaf
     Service.
     "Mexican Political Constitution: With
     Reforms and Up-To-Date Additions."

114. Doing Business in Mexico. Editor Susan
     K. Lefler. Albany: Matthew Bender, 1980.
     Loose-Leaf Service.
     "English Edition of the Anti-Trust Law."

SECONDARY MATERIAL: SERIALS

None

SECONDARY MATERIAL: MONOGRAPHS

None

Bankruptcy Laws

PRIMARY MATERIAL

115. Ley de Quiebras y de Suspension de Pagos
     (4-20-43).
     Law of Bankruptcy and Suspension of
     Payments.

LOCATION OF LEGISLATION

116. Codigo de Comercio y Leyes
     Complementarias. 45a ed. Mexico:
     Editorial Porrua, 1988.
     "Commercial Code and Complementary
     Laws."

117. Doing Business in Mexico. Editor Susan
     K. Lefler. Albany: Matthew Bender, 1980.
     Loose-Leaf Service.
     "English Edition of Bankruptcy Law."

118. Legislacion Mercantil. 2a ed. Mexico:
     Mexico Fiscal Laboral, S.A. de C.V.,
     1974-. Loose-Leaf Service.
     "Commercial Legislation."

119. Legislacion Mercantil y Leyes Conexas;
     Concordado con los de Alemania,
     Argentina, Chile, Espana, Francia e
     Italia. Mexico: Ediciones Andrade, 1976.

Loose-Leaf Service.
"Commercial Laws and Related Laws;
Concorded with Those of Germany,
Argentina, Chile, Spain, France and
Italy."

120. Ley de Quiebras y de Suspension de
Pagos. Mexico: Ediciones Andrade, 1979.
Loose-Leaf Service
"Law of Bankrupcy and Suspension of
Payments."

SECONDARY MATERIAL: SERIALS

None

SECONDARY MATERIAL: MONOGRAPHS

121. Cervantes Ahumada, Raul. Derecho de
Quiebras. 3a ed. Mexico: Editorial
Herrero, 1981.
"Bankruptcy Law."

122. Dominguez Del Rio, Alfredo. Quiebras:
Culpable, Fraudulenta: Ensayo Historico
Dogmatico.
"Fraud and Bankruptcy: A Historical and
Dogmatic Essay."

123. Ramirez Banos, Federico. Tratado de
Juicios Mercantiles. Mexico: Antigua
Liberia Robredo, 1963.
"Treatise on Mercantile Cases."

124. Rodriguez Rodriguez, Joaquin. La
Separacion de Bienes en la Quiebra.
Mexico: Imprenta Universitaria, 1978.
"The Award of Assets in the Bankruptcy
Proceedings."

Banks and Banking Laws

PRIMARY MATERIAL

125. Decreto Que Establece la Nacionalizacion de la Banca Privada (9-1-82).
Decree That Nationalized All Private Banks.

126. Ley de Sociedades de Inversion (1-14-85).
Law of Investment Companies.

127. Ley del Ahorro Nacional (12-30-50)(1-19-51).
National Savings Law.

128. Ley Federal de Instituciones de Fianza (12-29-50)(1-18-51).
Federal Law of Credit Institutions.

129. Ley General de Credito Rural (4-5-76).
General Law of Rural Credit.

130. Ley General de Organizaciones y Actividades Auxiliares del Credito (1-14-85).
General Law of Organizations and Activities Relating to Credit.

131. Ley General de Titulos y Operaciones de
     Credito (8-27-32).
     General Law of Securities and Credit
     Operations.

132. Ley Monetaria (7-27-31)(10-14-36).
     Currency Law.

133. Ley Organica de Nacional Financiera (12-
     26-86).
     Organic Law of the National Financier.

134. Ley Organica del Banco de Mexico
     (12-31-84).
     Organic Law of the Bank of Mexico.

135. Ley Organica del Banco Nacional de
     Comercio Exterior (1-20-86).
     Organic Law of the Export Bank.

136. Ley Organica del Banco Nacional de Obras
     y Servicios Publicos (1-20-86).
     Organic Law of the National Bank of
     Public Works and Services.

137. Ley Organica del Banco Nacional del
     Pequeno Comercio (1-20-86).
     Organic Law of the National Bank of
     Small Businesses.

138. Ley Reglamentaria del Servicio Publico
     de Banca y Credito (1-14-85).
     Regulatory Law of the Public Service of
     Banking and Credit.

LOCATION OF LEGISLATION

139. Commercial, Business and Trade Laws;
     Mexico. Compiled and Edited by Michael
     Wallace Gordon. Dobbs Ferry, New York:
     Oceana, 1983-. Loose-Leaf Service.

"English Edition of Securities Law and
Law of Instruments and Operations of
Credit."

140. Doing Business in Mexico. Editor Susan
K. Lefler. Albany: Matthew Bender, 1980.
Loose-Leaf Service.
"English Edition of Decree Nationalizing
the Banks of Mexico (9-2-82)."

141. Legislacion Bancaria: Ley General de
Instituciones de Credito y
Organizaciones Auxiliarias y
Disposiciones Complementarias. 32a ed.
Mexico: Editorial Porrua, 1988.
"Banking Legislation: General Law of
Institutions of Credit and Related
Organizations and Complementary
Legislation."

142. Legislacion Mercantil. 2a ed. Mexico:
Mexico Fiscal y Laboral, S.A. de C.V.,
1974-. Loose-Leaf Service.
"Commercial Legislation."

143. Legislacion Mercantil y Leyes Conexas:
Concordado con los de Alemania,
Argentina, Chile, Espana, Francia e
Italia. Mexico: Ediciones Andrade, 1974.
Loose-Leaf Service.
"Commercial Legislation and Related
Laws; Concorded with those of Germany,
Argentina, Chile, Spain, France and
Italy."

144. Ley General de Titulos y Operaciones de
Credito. 33a ed. Mexico: Editorial
Porrua, 1988.
"General Law of Securities and Credit
Operations."

145. <u>Tax Laws of the World: Mexico</u>. Alachua,
     Florida: Foreign Tax Law Association,
     1981-. Loose-Leaf Service.
     "English Edition of the Negotiable
     Instruments and Credit Operations Laws."

SECONDARY MATERIAL: SERIALS

146. "Doing Business in Mexico: The Impact of
     its Financial Crisis on Foreign
     Investors: A Symposium." <u>The
     International Lawyer</u> 18 (Spring 1984):
     285-329.

147. Gibbs, N. A. "Regional Bank's
     Perspective: An Analysis of the
     Differnce and Similarities in the U.S.
     Banking Community's Aproach to and
     Participation in the Mexican
     Restructuring." <u>Columbia Journal of
     Transnational Law</u> 23 (1984): 11-28.

148. Gomez Gordoa, J. "Algunos Aspectos de
     Nuestras Nuevas Disposiciones Legales en
     Materia Bancaria." <u>Revista de
     Investigaciones Juridicas</u> 11 (1987):
     305-317.
     "Some Aspects of Our New Legal
     Requirements Concerning Banking
     Matters."

149. Gouraige, Ghslain. "International
     Banking: Nationalization of Mexican
     Banks and Foreign Exchange Controls--The
     Nationalization Decree." <u>Harvard
     International Law Journal</u> 24 (Summer
     1983): 212-229.

150. Karon, Paul. "Law and Popular Credit in
     Mexico. "<u>Arizona Journal of
     International and Comparative Law</u> 1
     (Winter 1982): 88-121.

151. Munger, J.F. "Rights and Priorities of Secured Creditors of Personality in Mexico." <u>Arizona Law Review</u> 16 (1974): 767-797.

152. Ritch James E. "Legal Aspects of Lending to Mexican Borrows." <u>North Carolina Journal of International Law and Commercial Regulation</u> 7 (Summer 1982): 315-330.

153. Ritch, J.E. "Recent Developments in Mexican Legislation Affecting Banking and Finance." <u>Private Investors Abroad</u> (1983): 353-385.

SECONDARY MATERIAL: MONOGRAPHS

154. Acosta Romero, Miguel. <u>Derecho Bancario: Panorama del Sistem Financiero Mexicano</u>. 3a ed. Mexico: Editorial Porrua, 1986. "Banking Law: A Panorama of the Mexican Financial System."

155. Acosta Romero, Miguel. <u>La Banca Multiple</u>. Mexico: Editorial Porrua, 1981. "Multiple Banking."

156. Acosta Romero, Miguel. <u>Legislacion Bancaria: Doctrina, Compilacion Legal, Jurisprudencia</u>. 2a ed. Mexico: Editorial Porrua, 1989. "Banking Legislation: Doctrine, Legal Compilation, Jurisprudence."

157. Acosta Romero, Miguel. <u>La Nacionalizacion de la Banca Mexican, Proceso de Transformacion de las Sociedades Bancarias, Ensayo de Conceptuacion de las Sociedades Nacionales de Credito: Estudios Juridicos en Memoria de Roberto L.</u>

Mantilla Molina. Mexico: Editorial
Porrua, 1984.
"The Nationalization of the Banks, The
Transformation of the Banking
Corporations, A Conceptual Essay of the
Banking Corporations: Juridical Studies
in the Honor of Roberto L. Mantilla
Molina."

158. Arocha Morton, Carlos A. y Abelardo
Rojas Roldan. Leyes Bancarias:
Tematizadas y Comentadas. Mexico:
Editorial Porrua, 1986.
"Banking Laws: Arranged by Topic and
Annotated."

159. Astudillo Ursua, Pedro. Los Titulos de
Credito: Parte General. Mexico:
Editorial Porrua, 1983.
"Credit Instruments: General Part."

160. Barrera Graf, Jorge. Nueva Legislacion
Bancaria: Breves Comentarios Sobre las
Leyes del 14 de Enero de 1985. Mexico:
Editorial Porrua, 1985.
"New Banking Legislation: Brief
Commentaries on the Laws of January 14,
1985."

161. Bauche Garciadiego, Mario. Operaciones
Bancarias, Activas, Pasivas y
Complementarias. 5a ed. Mexico:
Editorial Porrua, 1985.
"Banking Operations, Active, Passive and
Complementary."

162. Berger S., Jaime B. <u>La Tarjeta de Credito y Su Aspectos Juridicos</u>. Mexico: Libreria Carrillo, 1981.
"The Credit Card and Its Legal Aspects."

163. Cervantes Ahumada, Raul. <u>Titulos y Operaciones de Credito</u>. 13a ed. Mexico: Editorial Herrero, 1984.
"Securities and Credit Operations."

164. Comision Nacional de Valores. <u>Los Bancos y el Mercado de Valores</u>. Mexico: Editorial Cultural, 1966.
"The Banks and the Stock Exchange."

165. Conchello, Jose Angel. <u>Devaluacion 82: El Principio del Fin</u>. Mexico: Editorial Grijalba, 1982.
"Devaluation of 1982: The Beginning of the End."

166. Garza, Sergio Francisco de la. <u>Derecho Financiero Mexicano</u>. 16a ed. Mexico: Editorial Porrua, 1990.
"Mexican Financial Law."

167. Giorgana Frutos, Victor Manuel. <u>Curso de Derecho Bancario y Financiero</u>. Mexico: Editorial Porrua, 1984.
"Study of Banking and Financial Law."

168. Gomez Gordoa, Jose. <u>Titulos de Credito</u>. Mexico: Editorial Porrua, 1988.
"Bill of Exchange."

169. Gonzalesz Bustamante, Juan Jose. <u>El Cheque: Su Aspectos Mercantiles y Bancarios, Su Tutela Penal</u>. 3a ed. Mexico: Editorial Porrua, 1974.
"The Check: Its Commercial and Banking Aspects, Its Criminal Tutelage."

170. Mantilla Molina, Roberto L. <u>Titulos de Credito Cambiarios: Letra de Cambio y Pagare</u>. 2a ed. Mexico: Editorial Porrua, 1983.
"Bills of Exchange: Promissory Notes."

171. Mejan, Luis Manuel C. <u>Secreto Bancario</u>. Bogota, Colombia: FELABAN, 1984.
"Banking Secrets."

172. Munoz, Luis. <u>El Fideicomiso</u>. 2a ed. Mexico: Cardenas, 1980.
"The Trust."

173. Pina Vara, Rafael de. <u>Teoria y Practica del Cheque</u>. 3a ed. Mexico: Editorial Porrua, 1984.
"Theory and Practice of the Check."

174. Ramirez, Miguel D. <u>Development Banking in Mexico: The Case of the Nacional Financiera, S.A.</u> New York: Praeger, 1986.

175. Rodriguez Rodriguez, Joaquin. <u>Derecho Bancario</u>. 3a ed. Mexico: Porrua, 1973.
"Banking Law."

176. Soto Subreyra y Silva, Ignacio. <u>La Nueva Ley Reglamentaria del Servicio Publico de Banca y Credito; Antecedentes y Comentarios</u>. 3a ed. Mexico: Editorial Porrua, 1987.
"New Regulatory Law on Public Banking and Credit: Antecedents and Commentary."

177. Tellez Ulloa, Marco Antonio.
     <u>Jurisprudencia Sobre Titulos y
     Operaciones de Credito: La Ley de
     Titulos y Operaciones de Credito con
     Jurisprudencia y Ejecutorias en su
     Articulado</u>. 2a ed. Mexico: Editorial del
     Carmen, 1980.
     "Jurisprudence on Securities and Credit
     Operations: The Law of Securities and
     Credit Operations with Jurisprudence and
     Articulated Court Decisions."

Civil Procedure Laws

PRIMARY MATERIAL

178. Codigo Federal de Procedimientos Civiles
     (2-24-44).
     Federal Civil Procedure Code.

179. Codigo de Procedimientos Civiles para el
     Distrito Federal (9-21-32).
     Civil Procedure Code for the Federal
     District.

LOCATION OF LEGISLATION

180. Codigo Federal de Procedimientos
     Civiles. Mexico: Ediciones Andrade,
     1940-. Loose-Leaf Service.
     "Federal Civil Procedure Code."

181. Codigo Federal de Procedimientos
     Civiles, Ley Organica del Poder Judicial
     Federal: Legislacion, Jurisprudencia,
     Doctrina. Miguel Acosta Romero y Genaro
     David Gongora Pimental. 2a ed. Mexico:
     Editorial Porrua, 1986.
     "Federal Civil Procedure Code, Organic
     Law of the Federal Judiciary:
     Legislation, Jurisprudence, Doctrine."

182. <u>Codigo de Procedimientos Civiles para el</u>
     <u>Distrito Federal.</u> 39a ed. Mexico:
     Editorial Porrua, 1990.
     "Civil Procedure Code for the Federal
     District."

183. <u>Nueva Legislacion de Amparo Reformado,</u>
     <u>Doctrina, Textos y Jurisprudencia,</u>
     <u>Codigo Federal de Procedimientos</u>
     <u>Civiles, Ley Organica del Poder Judicial</u>
     <u>Federal y Sus Reformas.</u> Alberto Trueba
     Urbina y Jorge Trueba Barrera. 49a ed.
     Mexico: Editorial Porrua, 1988.
     "New Legislation of the Reformed Writ of
     'Amparo' :Doctrine, Texts and
     Jurisprudence, Federal Civil Procedure
     Code, Organic Law of the Federal
     Judiciary and Its Reforms."

SECONDARY MATERIAL: SERIALS

184. Contreras Vaca, F.J. "Reformas y
     Adiciones Legislativas Correspondientes
     al Ano de 1988, Relativas al
     Reconocimiento de Validez y Ejecucion de
     Sentencias Extranjeras." <u>Revista de la</u>
     <u>Facultad de Derecho de Mexico</u> 39 no.
     163-165 (1989): 229-237.
     "Legislative Reforms and Additions
     Corresponding to 1988, Relative to
     Recognition and Enforcement of Foreign
     Judgments."

185. Fix-Zamudio, H. "Optimismo y Pesimismo
     en el Derecho Procesal Mexicano."
     <u>Revista de la Facultad de Derecho de</u>
     <u>Mexico</u> 38 no. 157-159 (1988): 59-111.
     "Optimism and Pessimism in the
     Procedural Law of Mexico."

186. Translosheros Peralta, C. "Un Nuevo
     Procedimiento Civil para el Distrito
     Federal." Revista de Investigaciones
     Juridicas 11 (1987): 515-523.
     "A New Civil Procedure for the Federal
     District."

SECONDARY MATERIAL: MONOGRAPHS

187. Acosta Romero, Miguel, y Genaro David
     Gongora Pimentel. Codigo Federal de
     Procedimientos Civiles, Ley Organica del
     Poder Judicial Federal: Legislacion,
     Jurisprudencia, Doctrina. 2a ed. Mexico:
     Editorial Porrua, 1986.
     "Federal Civil Procedure Code, Organic
     Law of the Federal Judiciary:
     Legislation, Jurisprudence, Doctrine."

188. Alcala-Zamora Y Castillo, Niceto.
     Derecho Procesal Mexicano. 2a ed.
     Mexico: Editorial Porrua, 1985.
     "Mexican Procedural Law."

189. Arellano Garcia, Carlos. Derecho
     Procesal Civil. 2a ed. Mexico: Editorial
     Porrua, 1987.
     "Civil Procedural Law."

190. Arellano Garcia, Carlos. Procedimientos
     Civiles Especiales. Mexico: Editorial
     Porrua, 1987.
     "Special Civil Procedures."

191. Arilla Bas, Fernando. Manual Practico
     del Litigante: Formulario y
     Procedimiento en Materia Civil y
     Mercantil. 5a ed. Mexico: Editores
     Mexicanos Unidos, 1971.
     "Practical Manual for the Practitioner:
     Formularies and Procedure for Civil and
     Commercial Matters."

192. Becerra Baustista, Jose. El Proceso
     Civil en Mexico. 12a ed. Mexico:
     Editorial Porrua, 1986.
     "Civil Procedure in Mexico."

193. Dorantes Tamayo, Luis. Elementos de
     Teoria General del Proceso. 3a ed.
     Mexico: Editorial Porrua, 1990.
     "General Elements of the Theory of
     Procedure."

194. Estrella Mendez, Sebastian. Estudio de
     los Medios de Impugnacion en el Codigo
     de Procedimientos Civiles para el
     Distrito Federal y la Procedencia del
     Juicio de Amparo. 2a ed. Mexico:
     Editorial Porrua, 1987.
     "Study of the Means of Appellate
     Procedure in the Civil Procedure Code
     for the Federal District and the
     Procedure for the Writ of 'Amparo'."

195. Gomez Lara, Cipriano. Derecho Procesal
     Civil. Mexico: Editorial Trillas, 1984.
     "Civil Procedure Law."

196. Medina, Rubens. Basic Elements of Due
     Process of Law in Mexico. Washington,
     D.C.: Library of Congress, 1976.

197. Obregon Heredia, Jorge. Codigo de
     Procedimientos Civiles para el Distrito
     Federal: Comentado Concordado y
     Contiene, Jurisprudencia, Tesis y
     Doctrina. 3a ed. Mexico: Editorial
     Porrua, 1987.
     "Civil Procedure Code for the Federal
     District: Annotated and Concorded, with
     Jurisprudence, Cases of Note and
     Doctrine."

198. Pallares, Eduardo. <u>Derecho Procesal Civil</u>. 4a ed. Mexico: Editorial Porrua, 1989.
"Civil Procedure Law."

199. Pallares, Eduardo. <u>Diccionario de Derecho Procesal Civil</u>. 18a ed. Mexico: Editorial Porrua, 1988.
"Dictionary of Civil Procedure."

200. Pallares, Eduardo. <u>Formulario de Juicio Civiles</u>. 17a ed. Mexico: Editorial Porrua, 1989.
"Formulary of Civil Cases."

201. Tellez Uloa, Marco Antonio. <u>El Enjuiciamiento Mercantil Mexicano: Comentarios, Doctrina, Jurisprudencia y Ejecutorias</u>. Guadalajara, Mexico: Ediciones Carillo Hermanos, 1973.
"Mexican Commercial Procedure: Commentaries, Doctrine, Jurisprudence and Decisions."

Commercial Laws

PRIMARY MATERIAL

202. Codigo de Comercio (10-1 to 13-1889).
Commercial Code.

203. Ley de las Camaras de Comercio y de las
de Industria (8-26-41).
Law of Chambers of Commerce and
Industry.

204. Ley de Navegacion y Comercio Maritimo
(11-21-63).
Law of Navigation and Maritime Commerce.

205. Ley Reglamentaria del Articulo 131 de la
Constitucion Politica de los Estados
Unidos Mexicanos en Materia de Comercio
Exterior (1-13-86).
Regulatory Law of Article 131 of the
Political Constitution of the United
Mexican States in Matters Relating to
Foreign Commerce.

206. Ley Sobre Atribuciones del Ejecutive
Federal en Materia Economica (12-30-
50).
Law of Prerogatives of the Federal
Executive in Economic Matters.

LOCATION OF LEGISLATION

207. <u>Codigo de Comercio y Leyes
     Complementarias</u>. 45a ed. Mexico:
     Editorial Porrua, 1988.
     "Commercial Code and Complementary
     Laws."

208. <u>Commercial, Business and Trade Laws:
     Mexico</u>. Compiled and Edited by Michael
     W. Gordon. Dobbs Ferry, New York:
     Oceana, 1983-. Loose-Leaf Service.
     "Commercial Code in English."

209. <u>Doing Business in Mexico</u>. Editor Susan
     K. Lefler. Albany: Matthew Bender, 1981.
     Loose-Leaf Service.

210. <u>Legislacion Mercantil</u>. Mexico: Mexico
     Fiscal Laboral, S.A. de C.V., 1974-.
     Loose-Leaf Service.
     "Commercial Legislation."

211. <u>Legislacion Mercantil y Leyes Conexas:
     Concordado con los de Alemania,
     Argentina, Chile, Espana, Francia e
     Italia</u>. Mexico: Ediciones Andrade, 1976.
     Loose-Leaf Service.
     "Commercial Legislation and Related
     Laws; Concorded with those of Germany,
     Argentina, Chile, Spain, France and
     Italy."

212. <u>Tax Laws of the World: Mexico</u>. Alachua,
     Florida: Foreign Tax Law Association,
     Inc. 1981-. Loose-Leaf Service.
     "Commercial Code in English."

SECONDARY MATERIAL: SERIALS

213. American Chamber of Commerce of Mexico.
     Business Mexico: A Comprehensive,
     Authorative Look at Today's Mexico and
     Its Economic, Investment and Trade
     Prospects. (1968-Present): Quarterly.

214. Barrera-Graf, Jorge. "The Vienna
     Convention on International Sales
     Contracts and Mexican Law: A Comparative
     Study." Arizona Journal of International
     and Comparative Law 1 (Winter 1982):
     122-165.

215. Kurth, Edward H. "Adjudicative
     Resolution of Commercial Disputes
     Between Nationals of the United States
     and Mexico." St. Mary's Law Journal 14
     (Summer 1983): 597-681.

216. Leon Tovar, S.H. "Codigo de Comercio,
     Decreto por el Que se Reforma Adicional
     y Derogan Diversas Disposiciones."
     Boletin Mexicano de Derecho Comparado 22
     (1989): 969-973.
     "Commercial Code, Decree that Repeals
     and Adds Various Provisions."

217. Miranda, F.R. "Foreign Companies
     Investing and Doing Business in Mexico-
     -Nationalization." The Business Lawyer
     28 (July 1973): 1217-1236.

218. Murphy, E.E. "Drafting Mexican-U.S.
     Commercial Agreements."The International
     Lawyer 5 (July 1971): 577-585.

219. Radway, R.J. "Doing Business in Mexico:
     A Practical Legal Analysis." The
     International Lawyer 14 (Spring 1980):
     361-376.

220. Schmitz, John W. "Profit Sharing in Mexico." Lawyer of the Americas 10 (Spring 1978): 99-116.

221. Smith, G.C. "The United States-Mexico Framework Agreement: Implications for Bilateral Trade." Law and Policy in International Business 20 (1989): 655-681.

222. Valencia Varrera, C.R., y R. Sanchez-Mejorada Velasco. "Fundamentals of Doing Business with Mexico: After the Exchange Controls." St. Mary's Law Journal 14 (1983): 683-707.

223. Witker, J. "Los Programas de Importacion Temporal para Producir Articulos de Exportacion (PITEX)." Boletin Mexicano de Derecho Comparado 22 (1989): 617-621.
"The Programs of Temporary Importation to Produce Articles for Exportation (PITEX)."

SECONDARY MATERIAL: MONOGRAPHS

224. Briseno Sierra, Humberto. El Arbitraje Comercial: Doctrina y Legislacion. Mexico: Editorial Limusa, 1988. "Commercial Arbitration: Doctrine and Legislation."

225. Cervantes Ahumada, Raul [et. al.]. Reforma de la Legislacion Mercantil. Mexico: Editorial Porrua, 1985. "Reforms of the Commercial Legislation."

226. Doing Business in Mexico. Editor Susan K. Lefler. Albany: Matthew Bender, 1981. Loose-Leaf Service.

227. Iturbide Galindo, Adrian. El Regimen de Capital Variable en las Sociedades Anonimas. Mexico: Editorial Porrua, 1985.
"The Legal Framework of the Stock Company."

228. Mantilla Molina, Roberto L. Derecho Mercantil: Introduccion y Conceptos Fundamentales, Sociedades. 25a ed. Mexico: Editorial Porrua, 1987.
"Commercial Law: Introduction and Fundamental Concepts, Companies."

229. Obregon Heredia, Jorge. Enjuiciamento Mercantil: Comentado y Concordado, Contiene Jurisprudencia, Tesis, Doctrina. 3a ed. Mexico: Editorial Porrua, 1987.
"Commercial Procedures: Commented and Concorded, with Jurisprudence, Cases of Note, Doctrine."

230. Organization of American States, General Legal Division. A Statement of the Laws of Mexico in Matters Affecting Business. 4th ed. Washington, D.C.: OAS, 1970.

231. Pallares, Jacinto. Derecho Mercantil Mexicano. Mexico: UNAM, 1987.
"Commercial Mexican Law."

232. Pina Vara, Rafael de. Elementos de Derecho Mercantil Mexicano. 20a ed. Mexico: Editorial Porrua, 1988.
"Elements of Mexican Commercial Law."

233. Puente y Flores, Arturo, y Octavio Calvo Marroquin. Derecho Mercantil. 30a ed. Mexico: Editorial Banca y Comercio, 1984.
"Commercial Law."

234. Ramirez Valenzuela, Alejandro. <u>Derecho
     Mercantil y Documentacion</u>. 7a ed.
     Mexico: Editorial Limusa, 1984.
     "Commercial Law and Documentation."

235. Soto Alvarez, Clemente. <u>Prontuatio de
     Derecho Mercantil</u>. Mexico: Editorial
     Limusa, 1985.
     "Memorandum of Commercial Law."

236. Tena, Felipe J. <u>Derecho Mercantil
     Mexicano: Con Exclusion del Maritimo</u>.
     12a ed. Mexico: Editorial Porrua, 1986.
     "Commercial Law: Excluding the Maritime
     Commercial Laws."

237. Weintraub, Sidney. <u>Free Trade Between
     Mexico and the United States?</u>
     Washington, D.C.: Brookings Institution,
     1984.

Constitutional Laws

PRIMARY MATERIAL

238. Constitucion Politica de los Estados
    Unidos Mexicanos (2-5-17)(2-6-17).
    Political Constitution of the United
    Mexican States.

239. Ley de Expropiacion (11-25-36).
    Expropriation Law.

240. Ley Organica del Congreso General de los
    Estados Unidos Mexicanos (5-25-79).
    Organic Law of the General Congress of
    the United Mexican States.

LOCATION OF LEGISLATION

241. Constitutcion Politica de los Estados
    Unidos Mexicanos. 83a ed. Mexico:
    Editorial Porrua, 1988.
    "Political Constitution of the United
    Mexican States."

242. Constitucion Politica de los Estados
    Unidos Mexicanos con Reformas y
    Adiciones al Dia. Mexico: Ediciones
    Andrade, 1965-. Loose-Leaf Service.

"Political Constitution of the United
Mexican States with Reforms and Up-To-
Date Additions."

243. <u>Constitution of Mexico, 1917 (as
amended)</u>. Washington, D.C.: General
Secretariat, Organization of American
States, 1972.

244. <u>Constitutions of the Countries of the
World</u>. Editors Albert P. Blaustein and
Gisbert H. Flanz. Dobbs Ferry, New York:
Ocean Publications, Inc., 1971-. Loose-
Leaf Service.

245. <u>Doing Business in Mexico</u>. Editor Susan
K. Lefler. Albany: Matthew Bender, 1981.
Loose-Leaf Service.

SECONDARY MATERIAL: SERIALS

246. Artega, E. "Los Tratados y las
Convenciones en el Derecho
Constitucional." <u>Revista de la Facultad
de Derecho de Mexico</u> 39 no. 163-165
(1989): 127-135.
"Treaties and Conventions and
Constitutional Law."

247. Bautista Rosas, Ramiro G. "The Need for
Constitutional Guarantees for the
Protection of Political Rights."
<u>National Lawyers Guild Practitioner</u> 44
(Summer 1987): 86-93.

248. Garcia Moreno, V.C. "Analisis del
Articulo 120 Constitucional." <u>Boletin
Mexicano de Derecho Comparado</u> 21 (1988):
827-836.
"Study of Article 120 of the
Constitution."

249. Martinez Bolle Goyri, V.M. "Desarrollo
     Historico Constitucional del los
     Derechos Humanos en Mexico." Boletin
     Mexicano de Derecho Comparado 22 (1989):
     913-931.
     "Constitutional Historical Development
     of Human Rights in Mexico."

250. "Mexican Law Symposium: The Contemporary
     Mexican Approach to Growth with Foreign
     Investment Controlled but Participatory
     Independence. M.W. Gordon: The Forbidden
     Zones in Mexico. V.A. Vilaplana: A
     Constitutional Comparison: Mexico, The
     United States and Uganda. F.N. Baldwin."
     California Western Law Review 10 (Fall
     1973): 1-104.

251. Perez de Acha, L.M. "El Articulo 29 de
     la Constitucion Federal." Revista de
     Investigaciones Juridicas 11 (1987):
     345-387.
     "Article 29 of the Federal
     Constitution."

252. Vasquez Pando, F.A. "Algunas Reflexiones
     Sobre la Constitucion Mexicana, a la
     Luz de Algunos Tratados Internacionales
     Sobre Derechos Humanos en Que Mexico es
     Parte." Revista de Investigaciones
     Juridicas 11 (1987): 525-553.
     "Some Thoughts on the Mexican
     Constitution, as it Relates to Some
     International Treaties on Human Rights
     to Which Mexico is a Party."

SECONDARY MATERIAL: MONOGRAPHS

253. Acosta Romero, Miguel [et al.]. La
     Reforma Municipal en la Constitucion.
     Mexico: Editorial Porrua, 1986.
     "Municipal Reform in the Constitution."

254. Acosta Romero, Miguel, y Genaro David
Gongora Pimentel. <u>Constitucion Politica
de los Estados Unidos Mexicanos:
Legislacion, Jurisprudencia, Doctrina:
Incluye las Reformas Constitucionales y
Legales Hasta el 7 de Febrero de 1984</u>.
3a ed. Mexico: Editorial Porrua, 1987.
"Political Constitution of the United
Mexican States: Legislation,
Jurisprudence, Doctrine: Including All
of the Reforms up to February 7, 1984."

255. Burgoa, Ignacio. <u>Derecho Constitucional
Mexicano</u>. 4a ed. Mexico: Editorial
Porrua, 1982.
"Mexican Constitutional Law."

256. Burgoa, Ignacio. <u>Diccionario de Derecho
Constitucional, Garantias y Amparo</u>.
Mexico: Editorial Porrua, 1984.
"Dictionary of Constitutional Law,
Guarantees and the Writ of 'Amparo'."

257. Carpizo, Jorge. <u>La Constitucion Mexicana
de 1917</u>. 7a ed. Mexico: Editorial
Porrua, 1986.
"The Mexican Constitution of 1917."

258. Carpizo, Jorge, y Jorge Madrazo.
<u>Congreso Nacional de Derecho
Constitucional: Memoria del III Congreso
Nacional de Derecho Constitucional</u>.
Mexico: UNAM, 1984.
"National Congress on Constitutional
Law: Minutes, III Congress."

259. Cueva, Mario de la. <u>Teoria de la
Constitucion</u>. Mexico: Editorial Porrua,
1982.
"Constitution Theory."

260. Madrid Hurtado, Miguel de la. Elementos
de Derecho Constitucional. Mexico:
Instituto de Capacitacion Politica:
Partido Revolucionario Institucional,
1982.
"Elements of Constitutional Law."

261. Madrid Hurtado, Miguel de la. Estudios
de Derecho Constitucional. 3a ed.
Mexico: Editorial Porrua, 1986.
"Constitutional Law Studies."

262. Martinez de la Serna, Juan Antonio.
Derecho Constitucional Mexicano. Mexico:
Editorial Porrua, 1983.
"Mexican Constitutional Law."

263. Noriega, C. Alfonso. La Naturaleza de
las Garantias Individuales en la
Constitucion de 1917. Mexico: UNAM,
1967.
"The Nature of the Individual Rights in
the Constitution of 1917."

264. Perez de Leon E, Enrique. Notas de
Derecho Constitucional y Administrativo.
11a ed. Mexico: Editorial Porrua, 1990.
"Annotations on Constitutional Law and
Administrative Law."

265. Polo Bernal, Efrain. Manual de Derecho
Constitucional. Mexico: Editorial
Porrua, 1985.
"Handbook on Constitutional Law."

266. Sayeg Helu, Jorge. Las Reformas y
Adiciones Constitucional Durante la
Gestion Presidencial de Miguel de la
Madrid. Mexico: Editorial Porrua, 1988.
"Constitutional Reform During Miguel de
la Madrid's Tenure as President."

267. Tena Ramirez, Felipe. <u>Derecho Constitucional Mexicano</u>. 23a ed. Mexico: Editorial Porrua, 1989.
"Mexican Constitutional Law."

268. Tena Ramirez, Felipe. <u>Leyes Fundamentales de Mexico, 1808-1983</u>. 15a ed. Mexico: Editorial Porrua, 1989.
"Fundamental Laws of Mexico, 1808-1983."

269. Valadez, Diego. <u>La Constitucion Reformada</u>. Mexico: Instituto de Investigaciones Juridicas, UNAM, 1987.
"The Reformed Constitution."

Consumer Laws

PRIMARY MATERIAL

270. Ley Federal de la Proteccion al
     Consumidor (12-22-75).
     Federal Consumer Protection Law.

LOCATION OF LEGISLATION

271. Codigo de Comercio y Leyes
     Complementarias. 45a ed. Mexico:
     Editorial Porrua, 1988.
     "Commercial Code and Related Laws."

272. Doing Business in Mexico. Editor Susan K
     Lefler. Albany: Matthew Bender, 1981-.
     Loose-Leaf Service.
     "English Edition of the Consumer
     Protection Law."

273. Ley Federal de Proteccion al Consumidor.
     13a ed. Mexico: Editorial Porrua, 1988.
     "Federal Consumer Protection Law."

274. Ley Federal de Proteccion al Consumidor.
     Mexico: Ediciones Andrade, 1976-. Loose-
     Leaf Service.
     "Federal Consumer Protection Law."

SECONDARY MATERIAL: SERIALS

275. Vargas, Jorge A. "An Overview of
Consumer Transactions Law in Mexico:
Substantive and Procedural Aspects." <u>New
York Law School Journal of International
and Comparative Law</u> 10 (Fall 1989): 345-
382.

SECONDARY MATERIAL: MONOGRAPHS

None

Contract Laws

PRIMARY MATERIAL

276. Codigo de Comercio: Libro 1 (10-1 to 10-13-18-89).
Commercial Code: Book 1.

277. Codigo Civil para el Distrito Federal, en Materia Comun, y Para Toda la Republica en Materia Federal:Libro 4 (3-26-28).
Civil Code for the Federal District, in Common Matters, and for the Entire Republic in Federal Matters: Book 4.

278. Ley Sobre el Contrato de Seguro (8-31-35).
Law of Insurance Contracts.

LOCATION OF LEGISLATION

279. Codigo Civil para el Distrito Federal. 56a ed. Mexico: Editorial Porrua, 1988. "Civil Code for the Federal District."

280. Codigo Civil para el Distrito Federal en Materia Comun y para Toda la Republica en Materia Federal Comentado. Mexico: Instituto de Investigaciones Juridicas, UNAM, 1990.

Civil Procedure Code for the Federal
District in Ordinary Matters and for the
Entire Republic in Federal Matters With
Commentary (Book 4)."

281. Codigo de Comercio y Leyes
Complementarias. 48a ed. Mexico:
Editorial Porrua, 1988.
"Commercial Code and Related Laws."

282. Commercial, Business and Trade Laws:
Mexico. Compiled and Edited by Michael
Wallace Gordon. Dobbs Ferry, New York:
Oceana Publications, Inc., 1983-. Loose-
Leaf Service.
"Commercial Code in English."

283. Legislacion Mercantil. Mexico: Mexico
Fiscal, 1974-. Loose-Leaf Service.
"Commercial Legislation."

284. Legislacion Mercantil y Leyes Conexas:
Concordado con los de Alemania,
Argentina, Chile, Espana, Francia e
Italia. Mexico: Ediciones Andrade, 1974.
Loose-Leaf Service.
"Commercial Legislation and Related
Laws: Concorded with those of Germany,
Argentina, Chile, Spain, France and
Italy."

285. Mexican Civil Code. Translated by
Michael Wallace Gordon. Dobbs Ferry, New
York: Oceana Publications, Inc., 1980.

286. Nuevo Codigo Civil para el Distrito
Federal en Materia Comun, y para Toda la
Republica en Materia Federal. Mexico:
Ediciones Andrade, 1938-. Loose-Leaf
Service.
"New Civil Code for the Federal District
in Ordinary Matters and for All of the
Republic in Federal Matters."

287. <u>Tax Laws of the World: Mexico</u>. Alachua,
     Florida: Foreign Tax Law Association,
     Inc., 1981-. Loose-Leaf Service.
     "Commercial Code in English."

SECONDARY MATERIAL: SERIALS

288. Leon Tovar, S.H. "El Contrato de
     Comision Mercantil." <u>Boletin Mexicano de
     Derecho Comparado</u> 21 (1988): 623-647.
     "The Commercial Commission Contract."

SECONDARY MATERIAL: MONOGRAPHS

289. Aguilar Carbajal, Leopoldo. <u>Contratos
     Civiles</u>. 3a ed. Mexico: Editorial
     Porrua, 1982.
     "Civil Contracts."

290. Arce Gargallo, Javier. <u>Contratos
     Mercantiles Atipicos</u>. Mexico: Editorial
     Trillas, 1985.
     "Atipical Commercial Contracts."

291. Bauche Garciadiego, Mario. <u>La Empresa:
     Nuevo Derecho Industrial, Contratos
     Comerciales y Sociedades Mercantiles</u>.
     Mexico: Editorial Porrua, 1983.
     "The Corporation: New Industrial Law,
     Commercial Contracts and Commercial
     Companies."

292. Bejarano Sanchez, Manuel. <u>Obligaciones
     Civiles</u>. 3a ed. Mexico: Harper & Row
     Latinoamericana, 1984.
     "Civil Obligations."

293. Borjas Soriano, Manuel. <u>Teoria General
     de las Obligaciones</u>. 11a ed. Mexico:
     Editorial Porrua, 1989.
     "General Theory of Obligations."

294. Munoz, Luis. _Teoria General del Contrato_. Mexico: Cardenas, 1973. "General Theory of Contracts."

295. Olivera de Luna, Omar. _Contratos Mercantiles_. 2a ed. Mexico: Editorial Porrua, 1987. "Business Contracts."

296. Pina, Rafael de. _Elementos de Derecho Civil Mexicano: Tomo 4 Contracts_. 6a ed. Mexico: Editorial Porrua, 1986. "Elements of Mexican Civil Law: Volume 4 Contracts."

297. Rojina Villegas, Rafael. _Compendio de Derecho Civil: Tomo 4 y 6 Contratos_. 18a ed. Mexico: Editorial Porrua, 1987. "Compendium of Civil Law: Volume 4 and 6 Contracts."

298. Sanchez Medal Urquiza, Jose Ramon. _De los Contratos Civiles: Teoria General del Contrato, Contratos en Especial, Registro Publico de la Propiedad_. 2a ed. Mexico: Editorial Porrua, 1988. "Civil Contracts: General Theory of Contracts, Special Contracts, Public Registry of Property."

299. Sanchez Medal Urquiza, Jose Ramon. _La Resolucion de los Contratos por Incumplimiento_. 3a ed. Mexico: Editorial Porrua, 1984. "Breach of Contract Resolutions."

300. Vasquez del Mercado, Oscar. _Contratos Mercantiles_. 3a ed. Mexico: Editorial Porrua, 1989. "Commercial Contracts."

301. Zamora y Valencia, Miguel Angel.
     <u>Contratos Civiles</u>. 2a ed. Mexico:
     Editorial Porrua, 1985.
     "Civil Contracts."

Copyright Laws

PRIMARY MATERIAL

302. Convencion Interamericana Sobre el
     Derecho de Autor en Obras Literarias
     (10-24-47).
     Inter-American Convention on Copyright
     in Literary, Scientific and Artistic
     Works.

303. Convencion Universal Derecho de Autor
     (6-6-57).
     Universal Copyright Convention.

304. Decreto por el Que se Promulga el Acta
     de Paris del Convenio de Bernas Para la
     Proteccion de las Obras Literarias y
     Artisticas (1-24-75).
     Decree Approving the Paris Action on the
     Berne Convention on Copyright.

305. Decreto por el Que se Promulga el Text
     de la Convencion de Bernas Para la
     Proteccion de las Obras Literarias y
     Artisticas (12-20-68).
     Decree Approving the Bern Convention on
     Copyright.

306. Decreto por el Que se Promulga la
     Convencion Sobre Propiedad Literaria y
     Artistica Suscrita en la Cuarta
     Conferencia Internacional Americana
     (4-23-63).
     Decree Approving the Inter-American
     Convention on Copyright.

307. Decreto por el Que se Promulga la
     Convencion Universal Sobre Derecho de
     Autor (3-9-76).
     Decree Approving the Universal Copyright
     Convention.

308. Ley Federal de Derechos de Autor
     (12-21-63).
     Federal Copyright Law.

LOCATION OF LEGISLATION

309. <u>Legislacion Sobre Derechos de Autor</u>. 8a
     ed. Mexico: Editorial Porrua, 1988.
     "Copyright Legislation."

310. <u>Nuevo Codigo Civil para el Distrito
     Federal en Materia Comun, y para Toda la
     Republica en Materia Federal</u>. Mexico:
     Ediciones Andrade, 1938-. Loose-Leaf
     Service.
     "Contains Copyright Law."

SECONDARY MATERIAL: SERIALS

311. Jacobsen, Mark P. "Mexico's Computer
     Decree: The Problem of Performance
     Requirements and a U.S. Response". <u>Law
     and Policy in International Business</u> 14
     (1983): 1159-1195.

312. Loredo Hill, A. "Letter From Mexico".
     <u>Copyright</u> 23 (1987): 300-303.

SECONDARY MATERIAL: MONOGRAPHS

313. Organization of American States: General
     Secretariat. <u>Copyright Protection in the
     Americas</u>. 4th ed. Dobbs Ferry, New York:
     Oceana, 1979.

314. Loredo Hill, Adolfo. <u>Derecho Autorial
     Mexicano</u>. Mexico: Editorial Porrua,
     1982. "Mexican Copyright Law."

Corporation Laws

PRIMARY MATERIAL

315. Codigo Civil: Libro 4, Titulo 11 (3-26-28).
     Civil Code: Book 4, Title 11.

316. Ley de Monopolios (8-31-34).
     Law of Monopolies.

317. Ley de Sociedades de Inversion (1-14-85).
     Law of Investment Companies.

318. Ley de Sociedades de Responsabilidad Mercantiles de Interes Publicos (8-31-34).
     Law of Commercial Companies of Public Interest.

319. Ley General de Sociedades Cooperativas (2-15-38).
     General Law of Cooperative Companies.

320. Ley General de Sociedades Mercantiles (8-28-34).
     General Law of Commercial Companies.

LOCATION OF LEGISLATION

321. Codigo Civil para el Distrito Federal.
     56a ed. Mexico: Editorial Porrua, 1988.
     "Civil Code for the Federal District."

322. Commercial, Business and Trade Laws:
     Mexico. Compiled and Edited by Michael
     Wallace Gordon. Dobbs Ferry, New York:
     Oceana Publications, Inc., 1983-. Loose-
     Leaf Service.
     "English Edition of the General Law on
     Commercial Companies."

323. Doing Business in Mexico. Editor Susan
     K. Lefler. Albany: Matthew Bender, 1988.
     Loose-Leaf Service.
     "English Edition of the General Law of
     Commercial Companies."

324. Legislacion Mercantil. 2a ed. Mexico:
     Mexico Fiscal y Laboral, S.A. de C.V.,
     1974-. Loose-Leaf Service.
     "Commercial Legislation."

325. Legislacion Mercantil y Leyes Conexas:
     Concordado con los de Alemania,
     Argentina, Chile, Espana, Francia e
     Italia. Mexico: Ediciones Andrade, 1974.
     Loose-Leaf Service.
     "Commercial Legislation and Related
     Laws; Concorded with those of Germany,
     Argentina, Chile, Spain, France and
     Italy."

326. Mexican Civil Code. Translated by
     Michael Wallace Gordon. Dobbs Ferry, New
     York: Oceana Publications, Inc., 1980.

327. Nuevo Codigo Civil para el Distrito
     Federal en Materia Comun, y para Toda la
     Republic en Materia Federal. Mexico:
     Ediciones Andrade, 1938-. Loose-Leaf
     Service.
     "New Civil Code for the Federal District
     in Ordinary Matters, and for All of the
     Republic in Federal Matters."

328. Sociedades Mercantiles y Cooperativas.
     42a ed. Mexico: Editorial Porrua, 1988.
     "Commercial Companies and Cooperative
     Companies."

329. Tax Laws of the World: Mexico. Alachua,
     Florida: Foreign Tax Law Association,
     Inc., 1981-. Loose-Leaf Service.
     "English Edition of the General Law of
     Commercial Companies."

SECONDARY MATERIAL: SERIALS

None

SECONDARY MATERIAL: MONOGRAPHS

330. Bauche Garciadiego, Mario. La Empresa:
     Nuevo Derecho Industrial, Contratos
     Comerciales y Sociedades Mercantiles.
     Mexico: Editorial Porrua, 1983.
     "The Company: New Industrial Law,
     Commercial Contracts and Commercial
     Company."

331. Frisch Philip, Walter. La Sociedad
     Anonima Mexicana. 2a ed. Mexico:
     Editorial Porrua, 1982.
     "The Mexican Stock Company."

332. Gaither, Roscoe Bradley. Handbook on
     Mexican Mercantile Law. Oberlin, Ohio:
     Academy Press, 1948.

333. Mantilla-Molina, Roberto. <u>Derecho Mercantil: Introduccion y Conceptos Fundamentales, Sociedades</u>. 24a ed. Mexico: Editorial Porrua, 1986. "Commercial Law: Introduction and Fundamental Concepts, Corporations."

334. Obregon Heredia, Jorge. <u>Enjuiciamiento Mercantil: Reforma al Codigo de Comercio del 4 de Enero de 1989, Comentado y Concordado, Contiene Jurisprudencia, Tesis, Doctrina</u>. 4a ed. Mexico: Editorial Porrua, 1990. "Commercial Adjudication: Reforms of the Commercial Code of January 4 of 1989, Annotated and Concorded, With Jurisprudence, Cases of Note, Doctrine."

335. Pallares, Eduardo. <u>Tratado Elemental de Sociedades Mercantiles</u>. Mexico: Antigua Libreria Robredo, 1965. "Basic Treatise on Commercial Companies."

336. Rodriguez Rodriguez, Joaquin. <u>Tratado de Sociedades Mercantiles</u>. 6a ed. Mexico: Editorial Porrua, 1981. "Treatise on Commercial Companies."

337. Vasquez del Mercado, Oscar. <u>Asambleas, Fusion y Liquidacion de Sociedades Mercantiles</u>. 3a ed. Mexico: Editorial Porrua, 1987. "Meetings, Mergers and Dissolutions of Commercial Companies."

Criminal Laws

343. Ley Organica de la Procuraduria General
     de la Republica (12-12-83).
     Organic Law of the Attorney General's
     Office of the Republic.

344. Ley Organica de la Procuraduria General
     de Justicia del Distrito Federal (12-
     12-83).
     Organic Law of the Attorney General's
     Office of the Federal District.

345. Ley Reglamentaria del Articulo 130 de la
     Constitucion Federal (1-18-27).
     Regulatory Law of Article 130 of the
     Federal Constitution.

LOCATION OF LEGISLATION

346. Codigo Penal para el Distrito Federal en
     Materia de Fuero Comun y para Toda la
     Republica en Materia de Fuero Federal.
     44a ed. Mexico: Editorial Porrua, 1988.
     "Criminal Code for the Federal District
     in Ordinary Matters and for the Entire
     Republic in Federal Matters."

347. Legislacion Penal Mexicana: Contiene,
     con Reformas Codigo Penal,
     Procedimientos Penales, Tribunales
     Federales, Comunes y de Menores,
     Ministerios Publicos, Cultos,
     Extradicion, Armas de Fuego y
     Explosivos, Defensorias de Oficio,
     Juegos Permitidos, Reglamentos, Etc.
     Mexico: Ediciones Andrade, 1938-.
     Loose-Leaf Service.
     "Criminal Legislation: Criminal Code,
     Criminal Procedures Code, and Other
     Related Legislation."

SECONDARY MATERIAL: SERIALS

348. Bernstein, Paul. "El Derecho y el Hecho:
     Law and Reality in the Mexican Criminal
     Justice System." Chicano Law Review 8
     (Annual 1985): 40-60.

349. Bunster, A. "Nuevas Reformas al Codigo
     Penal." Boletin Mexicano de Derecho
     Comparado 20 (1987): 857-873.
     "New Reforms to the Criminal Code."

350. Cardenas, Raul F. "Arrest and Detention
     in Mexico." International Commission of
     Jurists Review (June 1984): 58-62.

351. Gavin, John. "Mexico: The Drug
     Connection." Drug Enforcement 12 (Summer
     1985): 7-10.

352. "Mexico--A Profile." Drug Enforcement 12
     (Summer 1985): 11-18.

353. Miller, R.L. "Mexican Jails and American
     Prisoners." Louisiana Bar Journal 51
     (March 1976): 439-444.

354. Neal, J. Kennard. "United States-Mexican
     Relations 1981 Convention for Recovery
     and Return of Stolen Vehicles and
     Aircraft--Agreement Replaces 1936
     Convention and Clarifies Process for
     Recovery of Stolen Vehicles." Georgia
     Journal of International and Comparative
     Law 13 (Winter 1983): 143-157.

355. Rangel Medina, D. "Mexican Law of
     Obscenity." Lawyers of the Americas 7
     (June 1975): 337-348.

SECONDARY MATERIAL: MONOGRAPHS

356. Avalos, Francisco. Compilation of Treaties and Agreements in Force Relating to Narcotics Control Between Mexico and the United States as of December, 1984. Tucson, Arizona: University of Arizona College of Law Library, 1985.

357. Carranca y Trujillo, Raul. Codigo Penal Anotado. 12a ed. Mexico: Editorial Porrua, 1987.
"Annotated Criminal Code."

358. Carranca y Trujillo, Raul. Derecho Penal Mexicano, Parte General. 16a ed. Mexico: Editorial Porrua, 1986.
"Mexican Criminal Law: General Part."

359. Castellanos, Fernando. Lineamientos Elementales de Derecho Penal: Parte General. 27a ed. Mexico: Editorial Porrua, 1989.
"Basic Features of Criminal Law: General Part."

360. Diaz de Leon, Marco Antonio. Tratado Sobre las Pruebas Penales. 2a ed. Mexico: Editorial Porrua, 1988.
"Treatise on Criminal Evidence."

361. Garcia Ramirez, Sergio. La Reforma Penal de 1971. Mexico: Ediciones Botas, 1971.
"The Criminal Law Reform of 1971."

362. Gonzalez Blanco, Alberto. Delitos Sexuales en la Doctrina y en Derecho Positivo Mexicano. 4a ed. Mexico: Editorial Porrua, 1979.
"Doctrine and Mexican Positive Law on Sexual Crimes."

363. Gonzalez de la Vega, Francisco. El
     Codigo Penal Comentado: Puesto al Dia
     Conforme a sus Reformas y Concordado con
     la Jurisprudencia Definida de la Suprema
     Corte de Justicia de la Nacion y Sus
     Tesis Relacionadas. 9a ed. Mexico:
     Editorial Porrua, 1989.
     "The Annotated Criminal Code: Up-To-Date
     and Concorded with the Jurisprudence of
     the Supreme Court and with Related Cases
     of Note."

364. Gonzalez de la Vega, Francisco. Derecho
     Penal Mexicano: Los Delitos. 23a ed.
     Mexico: Editorial Porrua, 1990.
     "Mexican Criminal Law: Felonies."

365. Gonzalez Vidaurri, Alicia. Traslado
     Nacional e Internacional de
     Sentenciados. Mexico: Instituto Nacional
     de Ciencias Penales, 1985.
     "National and International Transfer of
     Convicted Criminals."

366. Hernandez Esparza, Abdon. El Delito de
     Defraudacion Fiscal: Estudio Dogmatico.
     Mexico: Ediciones Botas, 1962, Mexico.
     "The Crime of Tax Fraud: A Dogmatic
     Study."

367. Jimenez Huerta, Mariano. Derecho Penal
     Mexicano. 5a ed. Mexico: Editorial
     Porrua, 1985.
     "Mexican Criminal Law."

368. Ojeda Velazquez, Jorge. Derecho de
     Ejecucion de Penas. 2a ed. Mexico:
     Editorial Porrua, 1985.
     "The Execution of Prison Sentences."

369. Pavon Vasconcelos, Francisco. <u>Manual de Derecho Penal Mexicano: Parte General</u>. 7a ed. Mexico: Editorial Porrua, 1985. "Handbook of Mexican Criminal Law: General Part."

370. Perl, Raphael. <u>International Regulations of Narcotics Between the United States and Mexico</u>. Washington D.C: Library of Congress Law Library, 1976.

371. Porte-Petit Candaudap, Celestino. <u>Apuntamiento de la Parte General de Derecho Penal</u>. 12a ed. Mexico: Editorial Regina de Los Angeles, 1989. "Criminal Law Annotations of the General Section."

372. Porte-Petit Candaudap, Celestino. <u>Dogmatica Sobre los Delitos Contra la Vida y la Salud Personal: Estudio Comparativo con los Codigos Penales de las Entidades Federativas</u>. 8a ed. Mexico: Editorial Porrua, 1985. "Essay on the Crimes Against Life and Personal Health: A Comparative Study of the Criminal Codes of the Federal States."

373. Porte-Petit Candaudap, Celestino. <u>Ensayo Dogmatico Sobre el Delito de Violacion</u>. 5a ed. Mexico: Editorial Porrua, 1986. "Essay on the Crime of Rape."

Criminal Procedure Laws

PRIMARY MATERIAL

374. Codigo de Procedimientos Penales para el Distrito Federal (8-29-31).
Criminal Procedure Code for the Federal District.

375. Codigo Federal de Procedimientos Penales (8-30-34).
Federal Criminal Procedure Code.

376. Ley de Extradicion Internacional (12-29-75).
International Extradition Law.

377. Ley Reglamentaria del Articulo 119 de la Constitucion General de los Estados Unidos Mexicanos (1-9-54).
Regulatory Law of Article 119 of the General Constitution of the United Mexican States.

LOCATION OF LEGISLATION

378. Codigo de Procedimientos Penales. 38a ed. Mexico: Editorial Porrua, 1988.
"Criminal Procedure Code."

379. <u>Legislacion Penal Mexicana: Contiene,</u>
     <u>Con Reformas Codigo Penal,</u>
     <u>Procedimientos Penales, Tribunales</u>
     <u>Federales, Comunes y de Menores,</u>
     <u>Ministerios Publicos, Cultos,</u>
     <u>Extradicion, Armas de Fuego y</u>
     <u>Explosivos, Defesorias de Oficio, Juegos</u>
     <u>Permitidos, Reglamento, Etc</u>. Mexico:
     Ediciones Andrade, 1934-. Loose-Leaf
     Service.
     "Mexican Criminal Legislation: With
     Reforms to the Criminal Code, Criminal
     Procedure Code, Criminal Courts,
     Extradition, Fire Arms and Explosives,
     Permitted Gambling, Regulations, Etc."

SECONDARY MATERIAL: SERIALS

380. Fix-Zamudio, H. "Optimismo y Pesimismo
     en el Derecho Procesal Mexicano."
     <u>Revista de la Facultad de Derecho de</u>
     <u>Mexico</u> 38 no. 157-159 (1988): 59-111.
     "Optimism and Pessimism in the
     Procedural Law of Mexico."

SECONDARY MATERIAL: MONOGRAPHS

381. Briseno Sierra, Humberto. <u>El Articulo 16</u>
     <u>de la Constitucion Mexicana</u>. Mexico:
     UNAM, 1967.
     "Article 16 of the Mexican
     Constitution."

382. Colin Sanchez, Guillermo. <u>Derecho</u>
     <u>Mexicano de Procedimientos Penales</u>. 10a
     ed. Mexico: Editorial Porrua, 1986.
     "Mexican Criminal Procedure."

383. Diaz de Leon, Marco Antonio. Codigo
Federal de Procedimientos Penales
Comentado. Mexico: Editorial Porrua,
1988.
"Annotated Federal Criminal Procedure
Code."

384. Diaz de Leon, Marco Antonio. Diccionario
de Derecho Procesal Penal y de Terminos
Usuales en el Proceso Penal. Mexico:
Editorial Porrua, 1986.
"Dictionary of Criminal Procedure Law
and of Terms in Usage in the Criminal
Process."

385. Garcia Ramirez, Sergio. Curso de Derecho
Procesal Penal. 5a ed. Mexico: Editorial
Porrua, 1989.
"Criminal Procedure Course."

386. Garcia Ramirez, Sergio, y Victoria Adate
de Ibarra. Prontuario del Proceso Penal
Mexicano. 4a ed. Mexico: Editorial
Porrua, 1985.
"Memorandum Book of Mexican Criminal
Procedure."

387. Gonzalez Bustamante, Juan Jose.
Principios de Derecho Procesal Penal
Mexicano. 9a ed. Mexico: Editorial
Porrua, 1988.
"Principles of Criminal Procedure."

388. Martinez, Ernesto. Manual del Detenido:
Guia Legal de las Personas Privadas de
su Libertad. 3a ed. Mexico: EDAMEX,
1987.
"Handbook for the Jailed Person: Legal
Guide for People Deprived of Their
Liberty."

389. Obregon Heredia, Jorge. <u>Codigo de Procedimientos Penales para el Distrito Federal, Comentado y Concordado</u>. 4a ed. Mexico: Editorial Porrua, 1987. "Criminal Procedure Code for the Federal District, Annotated and Concorded."

390. Rivera Silva, Manuel. <u>El Procedimiento Penal</u>. 17a ed. Mexico: Editorial Porrua, 1988. "Criminal Procedure."

391. Zamora-Pierce, Jesus. <u>Garantias y Proceso Penal: El Articulo 20 Constitucional</u>. 4a ed. Mexico: Editorial Porrua, 1990. "Guarantees and Criminal Procedure: Constitutional Article 20."

Customs Laws

PRIMARY MATERIAL

392. Ley Aduanera (12-30-81).
     Customs Law.

393. Reglamento de la Ley Aduanera (6-18-82).
     Regulations of the Customs Law.

LOCATION OF LEGISLATION

394. Legislacion Aduanera. 9a ed. Mexico:
     Editorial Porrua, 1988.
     "Customs Legislation."

SECONDARY MATERIAL: SERIALS

395. Falcone, A.C. "Mexico's In-Bond
     Manufacturing Program: U.S. Tax
     Considerations after the 1986 Tax Act."
     Taxes: The Tax Magazine 65 (April 1987):
     211-220.

396. Roggensack, Meg. "United States
     Countervailing Duty Law as Applied to
     Mexico: The Need for a Material Injury
     Test." George Washington Journal of
     International Law and Economics 18
     (1984): 183-220.

SECONDARY MATERIAL: MONOGRAPHS

397. Carvajal Contreras, Maximo. <u>Derecho
     Aduanero</u>. Mexico: Editorial Porrua,
     1988.
     "Customs Law."

398. <u>Legal and Administrative Resolutions,
     Customs Bureau, In-Bond Industry</u>.
     Editors Patricia A. Sullivan and Maria
     Tellez-McGeach. Las Cruces, New Mexico:
     Joint Border Research Institute, 1987.

Domestic Relations Laws

PRIMARY MATERIAL

399. Codigo Civil: Libro 1 (3-26-28).
     Civil Code: Book 1.

LOCATION OF LEGISLATION

400. <u>Codigo Civil Para el Distrito Federal</u>.
     56a ed. Mexico: Editorial Porrua, 1988.
     "Civil Code for the Federal District."

401. <u>Codigo Civil para el Distrito Federal en
     Materia Comun y para Toda la Republic en
     Materia Federal Comentado</u>. Mexico:
     Instituto de Investigacion Juridica,
     UNAM, 1990.
     "Civil Code for the Federal District in
     Ordinary Matters and for the Entire
     Republic in Federal Matters With
     Commentary (Book 1 Persons, Book 3
     Successions)."

402. <u>Mexican Civil Code</u>. Translated by
     Michael Wallace Gordon. New York: Ocean
     Publications, Inc., 1980.

403. Nuevo Codigo Civil para el Distrito
Federal en Materia Comun, y para Toda la
Republica en Materia Federal. Mexico:
Ediciones Andrade, 1938-. Loose-Leaf
Service.
"New Civil Code for the Federal District
in Ordinary Matters, and for All of the
Republic in Federal Matters."

SECONDARY MATERIAL: SERIALS

404. "Divorce Law--Defective Mexican Divorce
Decree Accorded New York Recognition Due
to Subsequent Appearance, Through an
Attorney, of Party Absent From the
Mexican Action." Buffalo Law Review 20
(Fall 1970): 296-304.

405. Goddard, J.A. "El Poseedor Que Vendio
Bienes de la Herencia." Revista de
Investigaciones Juridicas 11 (1987): 11-
22.
"The Holder Who Sold Inheritance
Assets."

406. MacDonald Allen, D.G. "PS--We're
Divorced." Solicitors Journal 132
(August 1988): 1174-1176.

407. Ruiz Daza, M. "La Regulacion de Bienes
Entre Esposos." Revista de
Investigaciones Juridicas 11 (1987):
453-500.
"The Regulation of Assets Between
Spouses."

SECONDARY MATERIAL: MONOGRAPHS

408. Aguilar Carbajal, Leopoldo. Segundo
Curso de Derecho Civil: Bienes, Derechos
Reals y Sucesiones. 4a ed. Mexico:
Editorial Porrua, 1980.

"Second Course on Civil Law: Property, Federal Taxes and Successions."

409. Aguilar Gutierrez, Antonio. <u>Bases para un Anteproyecto de Codigo Civil Uniforme para Toda la Republica: Parte General, Derecho de la Personalidad, Derechos de Familia</u>. Mexico: UNAM, 1967.
"Bases for a Tentative Plan for a Uniform Civil Code for All of the Republic: General Section, Legal Capacity, Family Law."

410. Chavez Asencio, Manuel F. <u>La Familia en el Derecho: Derecho de Familia y Relaciones Juridicas Familiares</u>. Mexico: Editorial Porrua, 1987.
"The Family in the Law: Family Law and Its Juridical Capacities."

411. Chavez Asencio, Manuel F. <u>La Familia en el Derecho: Relaciones Juridicas Conyugales</u>. Mexico: Editorial Porrua, 1985.
"Family Law: The Conjugal Legal Relationship."

412. Galindo Garfias, Ignacio. <u>Derecho Civil: Primer Curso, Parte General, Personas, Familia</u>. 9a ed. Mexico: Editorial Porrua, 1989.
"Civil Law: First Course, General Part, Persons, Family."

413. Gastelum Gaxiola, Maria de los Angeles. <u>Agenda de Derechos y Obligaciones de la Mujer</u>. Mexico: Consejo Nacional de Poblacion, Comision Nacional de la Mujer, 1987.

414. Gutierrez y Gonzalez, Ernesto. El Patrimonio Pecunario y Moral: O Derecho de la Personalidad. Puebla, Mexico: J.M. Cajica Jr., 1971.
"Moral and Monetary Patrimony: Or the Law of Capacity."

415. Ibarrola, Antonio de. Cosas y Sucesiones. 6a ed. Mexico: Editorial Porrua, 1986.
"Estate Matters."

416. Ibarrola, Antonio de. Derecho de Familia. 3a ed. Mexico: Editorial Porrua, 1984.
"Family Law."

417. Martinez, Ernesto. Guia Legal de la Mujer: Manual Informativo para Que el Sexo Debil Conozca e Defienda Sus Derechos. 2a ed. Mexico: Editores Asociados Mexicanos, 1985.
"Legal Guide for the Women: Informative Manual So That the Weaker Sex Can Defend Their Rights."

418. Martinez Arrieta, Sergio Tomas. El Regimen Patrimonial del Matrimonio en Mexico. 2a ed. Mexico: Editorial Porrua, 1985.
"The Patrimony System of Marriage in Mexico."

419. Mayagoita Garza, Alberto. Matrimonio y Divorcio. Mexico: Panorama Editorial, 1984.
"Marriage and Divorce."

420. Montero Duhalt, Sara. Derecho de Familia. 2a ed. Mexico: Editorial Porrua, 1985.
"Family Law."

421. Pacheco, Alberto. <u>La Familia en el Derecho Civil Mexicano</u>. Mexico: Panorama Editorial, 1984.
"The Family in Mexican Civil Law."

422. Pallares, Eduardo. <u>El Divorcio en Mexico</u>. 5a ed. Mexico: Editorial Porrua, 1987.
"Divorce in Mexico."

423. Pina Vara, Rafael de. <u>Elementos de Derecho Civil Mexicanos</u>. 16a ed. Mexico: Editorial Porrua, 1989.
"Elements of Mexican Civil Law."

424. Rojina Villegas, Rafael. <u>Compendio de Derecho Civil</u>. 22a ed. Mexico: Editorial Porrua, 1988.
"Compendium of Civil Law."

425. Rojina Villegas, Rafael. <u>Derecho Civil Mexicano</u>. 7a ed. Mexico: Editorial Porrua, 1987.
"Mexican Civil Law."

Firearms Laws

PRIMARY MATERIAL

426. Ley Federal de Armas de Fuego y
     Explosivos (1-11-72).
     Federal Firearms and Explosives Law.

427. Reglamento de la Ley Federal de Armas de
     Fuego y Explosivos (5-6-72).
     Regulations of the Federal Firearms and
     Explosives Law.

LOCATION OF LEGISLATION

428. Legislacion Penal Mexicana: Contiene,
     con Reformas Codigo Penal,
     Procedimientos Penales, Tribunales
     Federales, Comun y de Menores,
     Ministerios Publicos, Cultos,
     Extradicion, Armas de Fuego y
     Explosivos, Defesorias de Oficio, Juegos
     Permitidos, Reglamento, Etc. Mexico:
     Ediciones Andrade, 1938-. Loose-Leaf
     Service.
     "Firearms and Explosives Law."

429. <u>Ley Federal de Armas de Fuego y Explosivos y Su Reglamento</u>. 14a ed. Mexico: Editorial Porrua, 1988. "Firearms and Explosives Law and Regulations."

SECONDARY MATERIAL: SERIALS

None

SECONDARY MATERIAL: MONOGRAPHS

None

Foreign Exchange Laws

PRIMARY MATERIAL

430. Decreto de Control de Cambio (12-13-82).
     Decree on Foreign Exchange.

431. Disposiciones Complementarias de Control
     de Cambio (5-11-87).
     Complementary Provisions of Foreign
     Exchange.

432. Ley Reglamentaria de la Fraccion 18 del
     Articulo 73 Constitucional en lo que se
     Refiere a la Facultad del Congreso para
     Dictar Reglas para Determinar el Valor
     Relativo de la Moneda Extranjera (12-
     27-82).
     Regulatory Law of Section 18 of
     Constitutional Article 73 in Reference
     to the Power of the Congress to
     Determine the Relative Value of Foreign
     Currency.

LOCATION OF LEGISLATION

433. Business Mexico: A Comprehensive,
     Authoritative Look at Today's Mexico and
     Its Economic, Investment and Trade
     Prospects. Mexico: American Chamber of
     Commerce of Mexico, 1967-.

"English Edition of the Exchange
Controls Decree, Volume 3, Number 1,
Page 102."

434. Doing Business in Mexico. Editor Susan
K. Lefler. Albany: Matthew Bender, 1980.
"English Edition of the Exchange Control
Decree."

435. Legislacion Bancria: Ley General de
Instituciones de Credito y
Organizaciones Auxiliarias y
Disposiciones Complementarias. 33a ed.
Mexico: Editorial Porrua, 1988.
"Banking Legislation: General Law of
Institutions of Credit and Related
Organizations and Complementary
Legislation."

436. Legislacion Mercantil y Leyes Conexas:
Concordado con los de Alemania,
Argentina, Chile, Espana, Francia e
Italia. Mexico: Ediciones Andrade, 1974.
Loose-Leaf Service.
"Commercial Legislation and Related
Laws: Concorded with Those of Germany,
Argentina, Chile, Spain, France and
Italy."

SECONDARY MATERIAL: SERIALS

437. "Doing Business in Mexico: The Impact of
its Financial Crisis on Foreign
Creditors and Investors: A Symposium."
International Lawyer 18 (Spring 1984):
285-329.

438. Gomez-Palacio, I. "Mexico's Foreign
Exchange Controls. Two Administrations
Two Solutions. Thorough and Benign."
University of Miami Inter-American Law
Review 16 (Fall 1984): 267-299.

439. Valencia, Carlos R., and Rodrigo Sanchez-Mejorada Velasco. "Fundamentals of Doing Business with Mexico: After the Exchange Controls." St. Mary's Law Journal 14 (Summer 1983): 683-707.

440. Vasquez Pando, Fernando A. "Legal Aspects of Mexican Exchange Controls." The International Lawyer 18 (Spring 1984): 309-321.

441. Zamora, S. "Exchange Controls in Mexico: A Case Study in the Application of IMF Rules." Houston Journal of International Law 7 (August 1984): 103-135.

442. Zamora, S. "Peso-Dollar Economics and Imposition of Foreign Exchange Controls in Mexico." American Journal of Comparative Law 32 (Winter 1984): 99-154.

SECONDARY MATERIAL: MONOGRAPHS

None

Foreign Investment Laws

PRIMARY MATERIAL

443. Ley Para Promover la Inversion Mexicana y Regular la Inversion Extranjera (3-9-73).
     Law to Promote Mexican Investment and Regulate Foreign Investments.

444. Ley y Reglamento de las Fracciones 1 y 4 del Articulo 27 Constitucional (1-21-26).
     Law and Regulations of Sections 1 and 4 of Article 27 of the Constitution.

445. Reglamento del Registro Nacional de Inversiones Extranjeras (12-28-73).
     Regulations of the National Registry of Foreign Investments.

446. Decreto Que Adiciona el Reglamento del Registro Nacional de Inversiones Extranjeras (8-23-79).
     Decree that Reforms the Regulations of the National Registry of Foreign Investments.

LOCATION OF LEGISLATION

447. Constitucion Politica Mexicana: Con
     Reformas y Adiciones al Dia. Mexico:
     Ediciones Andrade, 1935-. Loose-Leaf
     Service.
     "Mexican Political Constitution: With
     Reforms and Up-To-Date Additions.

448. Doing Business in Mexico. Editor Susan
     K. Lefler. Albany: Matthew Bender, 1980.
     Loose-Leaf Service.
     "English Edition of the Foreign
     Investment Law and Regulations".

449. Investment Laws of the World: Mexico.
     Dobbs Ferry, New York: Oceana
     Publications, Inc., 1973-. Loose-Leaf
     Service.
     "English Edition of the Foreign
     Investments Laws and Regulations."

450. Legislacion Sobre Propiedad Industrial,
     Transferencia de Tecnologia e
     Inversiones Extranjeras. 13a ed. Mexico:
     Editorial Porrua, 1988.
     "Legislation on Industrial Property,
     Transfer of Technology and Foreign
     Investments".

451. Tax Laws of the World: Mexico. Alachua,
     Florida: Foreign Tax Law Association,
     Inc., 1981-. Loose-Leaf Service.
     "English Edition of the Foreign
     Investments Law."

SECONDARY MATERIAL: SERIALS

452. Amador, Robert S. "Foreign Investment in
     Mexico." Antitrust law Journal 52 (Fall
     1983): 1017-1019.

453. American Chamber of Commerce. <u>Business
     Mexico: A Look at Today's Mexico and Its
     Economic, Investment and Trade
     Prospects</u>. Mexico: (1968-), Quarterly.

454. Bowen Robert E. and Timothy M.
     Hannessey. "Adjacent State Issues for
     the United States in Establishing an
     Exclusive Economic Zone: The Cases of
     Canada and Mexico." <u>Ocean Development
     and International Law</u> 15 (Fall 1985):
     355-375.

455. Bustamante, Eduardo A. and Zack V.
     Chayet. "The Mexican Maquilador
     Industry: Legal Framework of the
     1990's." <u>California Western
     International Law Journal</u> 20 (Spring
     1990): 263-273.

456. Calvo Nicolau, Enrique. "Mexican Taxes
     on Foreign Investment in Mexico."
     <u>Houston Journal of International Law</u> 12
     (Spring 1990): 265-290.

457. Camil, Jorge. "Mexico's 1989 Foreign
     Investment Regulations: The Cornerstone
     of a New Economic Model." <u>Houston
     Journal of International Law</u> 11 (Fall
     1989): 1-12.

458. "Centennial Feature: Law in Latin
     America. Preface. Introduction. P.T.
     Flawn: Expropriation and Aftermath: The
     Prospect for Foreign Enterprise in the
     Mexico of Miguel de la Madrid. E.E.
     Murphy; Mexico and the United States:
     The Need for Frankness. G.F. Margadant."
     <u>Texas International Law Journal</u> 18
     (Summer 1983): 427-474.

459. Clement, Norris C. "An Overview of the
Maquiladora Industry." California
Western International Law Journal 18
(Winter 1987): 55-64.

460. "Doing Business in Mexico: The Impact of
its Financial Crisis on Foreign
Creditors and Investors: A Symposium.
Preface. L.L. Brinsmade: Review
Perspective From An American Lawyer in
Mexico. J.C. Trevino: Legal Aspects of
Mexican Exchange Controls. F.A. Vazquez
Pando: The Nationalized Banking System
and Foreign Debts. J. Camil."
International Lawyer 18 (Spring 1984):
285-329.

461. Engle, Howard S. "Mexico's Maquiladora
Program: An Inviting Alternative for
U.S. Manufacturing." Tax Management
International Journal 14 (April 1985):
117-126.

462. Gomez-Palacio, Ignacio. "The New
Regulations on Foreign Investment in
Mexico: A Difficult Task." Houston
Journal of International Law 12 (Spring
1990): 253-263.

463. Gonzalez, Enrique A. "Franchising in
Mexico: Breaking With Tradition."
Franchise Law Journal 7 (Summer 1987):
3-6.

464. Gritsch, Norman R. "Mexico's
Maquiladoras Examined: Are In-Bond
Production Plants the Wave of the
Future?" Pepperdine Law Review 13
(January 1986): 357-385.

465. Hoagland, Alexander C. "Overview: Perspective From an American Lawyer in Mexico. (Symposium: Doing Business in Mexico: The Impact of Its Financial Crisis on Foreign Creditors and Investors)." The International Lawyer 18 (Spring 1984): 287-295.

466. Hodgins, David B. "Mexico's 1989 Foreign Investment Regulations: A Significant Step Forward, But is it Enough?" Houston Journal of International Law 12 (Spring 1990): 361-381.

467. Knight, John B. "Mexico Redoubles Effort to Attract Foreign Franchisors." Franchise Law Journal 9 (Spring 1990): 3-10.

468. Kozolchyk, Boris. "Commercial Legal Relations Between Arizona and Northern Mexico." Arizona Journal of International and Comparative Law Annual (1988):28-33.

469. Lucero Montano, M.A. "La Nueva Resolucion General Unica de la Comision Nacional de Inversiones Extranjeras." Revista de la Facultad de Derecho de Mexico 39 no. 163-165 (1989): 293-319. "The Only New General Resolution of the National Commission on Foreign Investments."

470. Machlowitz, David S. "Southward Ho: Relaxed Mexican Investment Laws Bring U.S. Firms Business." American Bar Association Journal 75 (Nov. 1989): 28(1).

471. Maviglia, Sandra F. "Mexico's Guidelines for Foreign Investment: The Selective Promotion of Necessary Industries." American Journal of International Law 80 (April 1986): 281-304.

472. Mihaly, Zooltan M. "New Business Opportunities in Mexico: Maquiladora Operations." Los Angeles Lawyer 12 (May 1989): 18-23.

473. Ogarrio, Alejandro and Leonel Pereznieto Castro. "Mexico-United States Relations: Economic Intergration and Foreign Investment (The New Environment for Trade and Investment in Mexico)." Houston Journal of International Law 12 (Spring 1990): 223-234.

474. Peters, Susanna. "Labor Law for the Maquiladoras: Choosing Between Workers' Rights and Foreign Investment (Mexican Labor Law From Three Perspectives)." Comparative Labor Law Journal 11 (Winter 1990): 226-248.

475. Ritch, James E. Jr. "The Regulation of Forcign Business in Mexico: Recent Legislation in Historical Perspective." North Carolina Journal of International Law and Commercial Regulation 7 (Summer 1982): 315-330.

476. Rojas, V.H. "New Foreign Investment Regulations of Mexico." International Business Lawyer 18 (1990): 135-139.

477. Sanchez Ugarte, Fernando. "Mexico's New Foreign Investment Climate." Houston Journal of International Law 12 (Spring 1990): 243-252.

478. "Seminar on the Law of Real Property
     Acquisition in Mexico: Introduction to
     Investment in Real Property in Mexico:
     An Overview of Constitutional and
     Statutory Restrictions. G. Gutierrez
     Quiroz: An Introduction to Secured Real
     Estate Transactions in Mexico. O. Rivera
     Faber: The Mexican Land Registry: A
     Critical Evaluation. B. Kozolchyk: The
     Mexican Mining Concession--Its Features,
     Regulation and Pracice. G.J. Perez: A
     Selected Bibliography on Mexican Real
     Property Law. E.L. Revilla." Arizona Law
     Review 12 (Summer 1970): 265-389.

479. Smith, William and Eduardo Vazquez
     Pando. "Effective Tax Planning for
     Mexican Operations (Oil, Gas and Related
     Industries)." Oil and Gas Tax Quarterly
     29 (June 1981): 309-321.

480. Tarbox, John E. "An Investor's
     Introduction to Mexico's Maquiladora
     Program." Texas International Law
     Journal 22 (Winter 1987): 109-139.

481. Trevino, Julio C. "Mexico: The Present
     Status of Legislation and Government
     Policies on Direct Foreign Investment."
     The International Lawyer 18 (Spring
     1984): 297-308.

482. Turro, John. "Mexican Maquiladoras
     Provide Backdoor to U.S. Market." Tax
     Notes International 2 (Oct. 1990): 1013-
     1015.

483. Valencia Barrera, Carlos R.
     "Fundamentals of Doing Business with
     Mexico: After the Exchange Controls."
     St. Mary's Law Journal 14 (Summer 1983):
     683-707.

484. Witker, J. "Nuevo Reglamento Sobre
     Inversiones Extranjeras." Boletin
     Mexicano de Derecho Comparado 22 (1989):
     975-979.
     "New Regulations on Foreign
     Investments."

485. Wobeser, Claus von and Kathleen
     Burguete. "New Mexican Foreign
     Investment Regulations." International
     Business Lawyer 17 (Dec. 1989): 519-
     523.

SECONDARY MATERIAL: MONOGRAPHS

486. Carrillo V., Jorge y Alberto Hernandez
     H. La Industria Maquiladora en Mexico:
     Bibliografia, Directorio e
     Investigaciones Recientes. La Jolla,
     California: University of California,
     1981.
     "The 'Maquiladora' Industry in Mexico:
     Bibliography, Directory and Recent
     Investigations."

487. Doing Business in Mexico. New York:
     Price Waterhouse, 1990.

488. Doing Business in Mexico. Editor Susan
     K. Lefler. Albany: Matthew Bender, 1980.
     Loose-Leaf Service.

489. Foreign Investment, Legal Framework and
     Its Application. Edited by the Comision
     Nacional de Investigaciones Extranjeras,
     in Coordination with the Direccion
     General de Comunicacion Social de la
     Presidencia de la Republica. Mexico:
     National Commission of Foreign
     Investment, 1986.

490. Federal Bar Association. <u>U.S.-Mexico Trade and Investment Law Conference</u>. Washington, D.C.: Federal Bar Association, 1982.

491. Gomez Palacio y Gutierrez Zamora, Ignacio. <u>Inversion Extranjera Directa</u>. Mexico: Editorial Porrua, 1985. "Direct Foreign Investment."

492. Gordon, Michael. <u>Mexican and Guatemalan Constitutional Provisions, Laws and Other Documents Relating to Foreign Trade and Investment</u>. 3rd ed. Gainesville, Florida: College of Law, University of Florida, 1979.

493. Organization of American States, General Legal Division. <u>A Statement of the Laws of Mexico in Matters Affecting Business</u>. 4th ed. Washington, D.C.: Organization of American States, 1970.

494. Radway, Robert J. <u>Joint Ventures in Mexico</u>. New York: AMA Membership Publications Division, American Management Association, 1984.

495. Ramos Garza, Oscar. <u>Mexico Ante la Inversion Extranjera: Legislacion, Politicas y Practicas</u>. 3a ed. Mexico: Docal Editorial, 1974. "Mexico Faces Foreign Investment: Legislation, Policies, and Practices."

496. Schmidt, Klaus D. <u>Doing Business in Mexico</u>. Menlo Park, California: SRI, 1980.

497. Sklair, Leslie. <u>Maquiladoras: Annotated Bibliography and Research Guide to Mexico's In-Bond Industry, 1980-1988</u>. [San Diego]: University of California, San Diego, 1988.

498. Weintraub, Sidney. <u>Free Trade Between Mexico and the United States?</u> Washington, D.C.: Brookings Institute, 1984.

Foreign Judgment Recognition

PRIMARY MATERIAL

499. Codigo de Procedimientos Civiles para el
     Distrito Federal: Capitulo 5, Seccion 4,
     Articulos 599-608 (9-21-32).
     Civil Procedure Code for the Federal
     District: Chapter 5, Section 4, Articles
     599-608.

500. Codigo Federal de Procedimientos
     Civiles: Libro 4, Titulo Unico, Capitulo
     1-4, Articulos 543-577 (2-24-42).
     Federal Civil Procedure Code: Book 4,
     Sole Title, Chapters 1-4, Articles 543-
     577.

LOCATION OF LEGISLATION

501. Codigo de Procedimientos Civiles para el
     Distrito Federal. 32a ed., Mexico:
     Editorial Porrua, 1986.
     "Civil Procedure Code for the Federal
     District."

502. Codigo Federal de Procedimientos
     Civiles. Mexico: Ediciones Andrade,
     1940-. Loose-Leaf Service.
     "Federal Civil Procedure Code."

503. <u>Codigo Federal de Procedimientos
     Civiles, Ley Organica de Poder Judicial
     Federal: Legisalcion, Jurisprudencia,
     Doctrina.</u> Miguel Acosta Romero y Genaro
     David Gongora Pimentel. Mexico:
     Editorial Porrua, 1983.
     "Federal Civil Procedure Code, Organic
     Law of the Federal Judiciary:
     Legisaltion, Jurisprudence, Doctrine."

504. <u>Nueva Legislacion de Amparo Reformado,
     Doctrina, Textos y Jurisprudencia:
     Codigo Federal de Procedimientos
     Civiles, Ley Organica del Poder Judicial
     Federal y Sus Reformas.</u> Alberto Trueba
     Urbina y Jorge Trueba Barrera. 49a ed.,
     Mexico: Editorial Porrua, 1988.
     "New Legislation of the Reformed Writ of
     'Amparo', Doctrine, Text and
     Jurisprudence: Federal Civil Procedure
     Code, Organic Law of the Federal
     Judiciary and Reforms."

SECONDARY MATERIAL: SERIALS

505. Cohen, Mitchell M. and Martha L.
     Hutzelman. "Interamerican Cooperation in
     Obtaining Testimony: The Problem of
     Intergrating Foreign Systems of
     Evidence: A Comparative Study of the
     United States, the Federal Republic of
     Germany, and Mexico." <u>Lawyer of the
     Americas</u> (Summer 198): 211-234.

506. Contreras Vaca, F.J. "Reformas y
     Adiciones Legislativas Correspondientes
     al Ano de 1988, Relativas al
     Reconocimiento de Validez y Ejecucion de
     Sentencias Extranjeras." <u>Revista de la
     Facultad de Derecho de Mexico</u> 39 no.
     163-165 (1989): 229-237.

"Legislative Reforms and Additions Corresponding to 1988, Relative to the Recognition and Enforcement of Foreign Judgments."

507. Garcia Moreno, V.C. "Reformas de 1988 en Materia de Cooperacion Procesal Internacional." Revista de la Facultad de Derecho de Mexico 39 no. 163-165 (1989): 345-368.
"1988 Reforms Concerning International Procedural Cooperation."

508. Siqueiros, Jose Luis. "Enforcement of Foreign Civil and Commercial Judgments in the Mexican Republic". Houston Journal of International Law 2 (Spring 1980): 375-385.

509. "Transcripts of the Symposium on Judicial Cooperation Between the United States and Mexico: Service of Process; Taking of Evidence; Enforcement of Foreign Judgments; Judicial Cooperation in Penal Matters." Arizona Journal of International and Comparative Law (1985 Annual): 1-255.

SECONDARY MATERIAL: MONOGRAPHS

510. Avalos, Francisco. Enforcement of United States Civil Court Judgments in Mexico: A Selective Bibliography. Tucson, Arizona: University of Arizona College of Law, 1984.

Health and Environment Laws

PRIMARY MATERIAL

511. Codigo Sanitario de los Estados Unidos
Mexicanos (3-13-73).
Sanitary Code of the United Mexican
States.

512. Ley de Salud para el Distrito Federal
(1-15-87).
Health Law for the Federal District.

513. Ley Federal de Proteccion al Ambiente
(1-11-82).
Federal Environmental Protection Law.

514. Ley General del Equilibrio Ecologico y
la Proteccion Ambiental (1-28-88).
General Law of Ecological Balance and
Environmental Protection.

515. Regalmento de la Ley General del
Equilibrio Ecologico y la Proteccion al
Ambiente en Materia de Impacto Ambiental
(6-7-88).
Regulations of the General Law of
Ecological Balance and Environmental
Protection in Matters of Evironmental
Impact.

516. Reglamento de la Ley General del Equilibrio Ecologico y la Proteccion al Ambiente en Materia de Prevencion y Control de la Contaminacion de la Atmosfera (12-25-88).
"Regulations of the General Law of Ecological Balance and Environmental Protection in Matters of Prevention and Control of Atmosphere Pollution.

517. Reglamento para la Prevencion y Control de la Contaminacion de Aguas (3-29-73).
"Regulations for the Prevention of Water Pollution."

LOCATION OF LEGISLATION

518. <u>Codificacion Sanitaria Mexicana</u>. Mexico: Ediciones Andrade, 1965-. Loose-Leaf Service.
"Mexican Health Code."

519. <u>Codigo Sanitario y Sus Disposiciones Reglamentarias</u>. 18a ed. Mexico: Editorial Porrua, 1982.
"Sanitary Code and Related Regulatory Provisions."

520. <u>Doing Business in Mexico</u>. Editor Susan K. Lefler. Albany: Matthew Bender, 1980. Loose-Leaf service
"English Edition of the Federal Environmental Protection Law."

521. <u>Ley Federal de Proteccion al Ambiente</u>. Mexico: Editorial Porrua, 1986.
"Federal Environmental Protection Law."

SECONDARY MATERIAL: SERIALS

522. Barnett, Barry C. "Transnational
Pollution: Agreement Regarding Marine
Pollution Incidents-Agreement of
Cooperation Between the United States of
America and the United Mexican States
Regarding Pollution of the Marine
Environment by Discharge of Hydrocarbons
and Other Hazardous Substances." Harvard
International Law Journal 23 (Spring
1982): 177-185.

523. Dumars, Charles T. and Salvador Beltran
del Rio M. "A Survey of the Air and
Water Quality Laws of Mexico." Natural
Resources Journal 28 (Fall 1988): 787-
813.

524. Glover, Nancy J. "The New River: The
Possibility of Criminal Liability for
Transnational Pollution." Criminal
Justice Journal 10 (Fall 1987): 99-119.

525. Hagost, Scott A. "U.S.-Mexico
Environmental Cooperation: Agreement
Between the United States of America and
the United Mexican States on Cooperation
for the Protection and Improvement of
the Environment in the Border Area."
Environmental Law Quarterly Newsletter
(Spring 1984): 1-3.

526. "Mexican Law Symposium. The Juridical
Regulation of Transnational Enterprises.
J.L. Siqueiros: Legal Protection of the
Environment in Mexico. L. Cabrera
Acevedo: Linking Foreign With Mexican
Trademarks: Boon or Bane?. D.W. James:

Legal Aspects of Activities of Foreign Finacial Institutions in Mexico. J.E. Ritch: Defining New Lines of Products Under Mexico's Foreign Investment Law. I Gomez-Palacio." <u>California Western International Law Journal</u> 8 (Winter 1978): 1-92.

527. "Mexico-United States: Agreement to Cooperate in the Solution of Environmental Problems in the Border Area." <u>International Legal Materials</u> 22 (September 1983): 1025-1032.

528. Nalven, Joseph. "Transboundary Environmental Problems Solving: Social Process, Cultural Perception." <u>Natural Resources Journal</u> 26 (Fall 1986): 793-832.

529. Rose, Elizabeth C. "Transboundary Harm: Hazardous Waste Management Problems and Mexico's Maquiladoras." <u>International Lawyer</u> 23 (Spring 1989): 223-244.

530. Shavelson, Lonny. "Acid River: Mexican Industry is Polluting California Waters." <u>California Lawyer</u> 9 (Oct. 1989): 24(2).

531. Sinclair, Mark A. "The Environmental Cooperation Agreement Between Mexico and the United States: A Response to the Pollution Problems of the Borderlands." <u>Cornell International Law Journal</u> 19 (Winter 1986): 87-142.

532. Sullivan, Margaret M. "Transboundary Pollution From Mexico: Is Judicial Relief Provided by International Principles of Tort Law?" <u>Houston Journal of International Law</u> 10 (August 1987): 105-131.

533. Tolivia, Enrique. "Problemas y
Perspectivas de la Calidad del Aire en
la Frontera." <u>Natural Resources Journal</u>
22 (Oct. 1982): 1141-1146.
"Problems and Perspectives of the
Quality of the Air on the Border."

534. U.S. Department of State. "Mexico-United
States: Agreement to Cooperate in the
Solution of Environmental Problems in
the Border Area." <u>International Legal
Materials</u> 22 (September 1983):
1025-1032.

535. Weston, Scott N. "United States-Mexico:
Coping with Environmental Problems at
the Border." <u>Loyola of Los Angeles
International and Comparative Law
Journal</u> 9 (Fall 1986): 117-136.

SECONDARY MATERIAL: MONOGRAPHS

536. Diaz, Luis Miguel. <u>Responsabilidad del
Estado y Contaminacion</u>. Mexico:
Editorial Porrua, 1982.
"State Responsibility and Pollution."

537. Marco del Pont, Luis. <u>El Crimen de
Contaminacion</u>. 2a ed. Mexico: Editorial
Villicana, 1986.
"The Crime of Environmental Pollution."

Housing and Urban Development Laws

PRIMARY MATERIAL

538. Ley del Desarrollo Urbano del Distrito
     Federal (1-7-76).
     Urban Development Law for the Federal
     District.

539. Ley Federal de Vivienda (2-7-84).
     Federal Housing Law.

540. Ley General de Asentamientos Humanos
     (5-26-76).
     General Law of Human Population Centers.

541. Ley General de Poblacion (1-7-74).
     General Law of Population.

542. Ley Sobre el Regimen de Propiedad en
     Condominio de Inmuebles, para el
     Distrito Federal (12-28-72).
     Law on Condominium Propery for the
     Federal District.

LOCATION OF LEGISLATION

543. Extranjeria Turismo y Poblacion. 3a ed.
     Mexico: Ediciones Andrade, 1973-. Loose-
     Leaf Service.
     "Alienage Tourism and Population."

544. Ley General de Asentamientos Humanos.
Mexico: Ediciones Andrade, 1976-. Loose-
Leaf Service.
"General Law of Human Population
Centers."

545. Ley General de Asentamientos Humanos:
Ley del Desarrollo Urbano del Distrito
Federal: Ley Federal de Viviendas y
Disposiciones Complementarias. 9a ed.
Mexico: Editorial Porrua, 1988.
"General Law of Human Population
Centers; Urban Development Law of the
Federal District; Federal Housing Law
and Related Legislation."

SECONDARY SOURCES: SERIALS

546. Armienta Calderon, G.M. "Ultimas
Reformas en Materia de Arrendamiento en
el Distrito Federal." Revista de la
Facultad de Derecho de Mexico 38 no.
157-159 (1988): 1-16.
"Latest Reforms on Matters Concerning
Leasing and Renting in the Federal
District."

547. Carmona Lara, M. "Reflexiones para el
Establecimiento de un Codigo Urbano para
el Distrito Federal." Boletin Mexicano
de Derecho Comparado 20 (1987): 875-
885.
"Some Thoughts on Establishing a Urban
Code for the Federal District."

548. Eibenschutz, Roberto. "La Planeacion del
Desarrollo Urbano (Symposium on
Anticipating Transboundary Resources
Needs and Issues in the U.S.-Mexico
Border Region)." Natural Resources
Journal 22 (October 1982): 797-803.
"Planning Urban Development."

SECONDARY SOURCES: MONOGRAPHS

None

Insurance Laws

PRIMARY MATERIAL

549. Ley General de Instituciones de Seguro
     (9-12-35).
     General Law of Insurance Companies.

550. Ley Sobre el Contrato de Seguro (8-31-
     35).
     Law on Insurance Contracts.

551. Reglamento de Agentes de Seguro (9-8-
     81).
     Regulations for Insurance Agents.

552. Seguro del Viajero (9-2-88).
     Travelers Insurance (On Public
     Transport).

LOCATION OF LEGISLATION

553. Codigo de Comercio y Leyes
     Complementarias. 45a ed. Mexico:
     Editorial Porrua, 1988.
     "Commercial Code and Complementary
     Laws."

554. Seguros y Fianzas: Ley General de
     Instituciones de Seguros, Ley Sobre el
     Contrato de Seguro, Ley Federal de
     Instituciones de Fianzas y Disposiciones
     Complementarias. 20a ed. Mexico:
     Editorial Porrua, 1987.
     "Insurance and Bonds: General Law of
     Insurance Companies, Law of Insurance
     Contracts, Federal Law of Bond
     Institutions and Complementary
     Provisions."

555. Tax Laws of the World: Mexico. Alachua,
     Florida: Foreign Tax Law Association,
     Inc., 1981-. Loose-Leaf Service.
     "English Edition of the General Law of
     Insurance Companies."

SECONDARY MATERIAL: SERIALS

556. Estrella, O. "Insurance in Mexico with
     an Emphasis on Autombile Insurance".
     Forum 17 (Winter 1982): 745-762.

557. Gomez Gordoa, J. "La Institucion
     Juridica del Seguro en Mexico." Revista
     de Investigaciones Juridicas 12 (1988):
     133-140.
     "The Legal Framework of Insurance in
     Mexico."

SECONDARY MATERIAL: MONOGRAPHS

558. Martinez Gil, Jose de Jesus. Manual
     Teorico y Practico de Seguros. Mexico:
     Editorial Porrua, 1984.
     "Handbook on the Theory and Practice of
     Insurance."

559. Seguros y Fianzas. 21a ed. Mexico:
     Editorial Porrua, 1988.
     "Insurance Surety and Fidelity."

Labor Laws

PRIMARY MATERIAL

560. Ley de Compensaciones de Emergencia al
Salario Insuficiente (9-24-43).
Emergency Compensation Law for
Insufficient Salary.

561. Ley Federal de los Trabajadores al
Servicio del Estado (12-28-63).
Federal Civil Servant Labor Law.

562. Ley Federal del Trabajo (4-1-70).
Federal Labor Law.

563. Mexico is also a signator to many
International Labor Conventions.

LOCATION OF LEGISLATION

564. Commercial, Business and Trade Laws:
Mexico. Compiled and Edited by Michael
Wallace Gordon. Dobbs Ferry: Oceana
Publications, Inc., 1983-. Loose-Leaf
Service.
"Federal Labor Code in English."

565. <u>Legislacion Sobre Trabajo</u>. Mexico:
Ediciones Andrade, 1937-. Loose-Leaf
Service.
"Labor Legislation."

566. <u>Ley Federal del Trabajo: Con Una</u>
<u>Explicacion Sencilla de los Articulos</u>
<u>para Su Mejor Compresion</u>. Mexico:
Trillas, 1986.
"Federal Labor Law with Notes for Easy
Understanding."

567. <u>Legislacion Federal del Trabajo</u>
<u>Burocratico: Comentarios y</u>
<u>Jurisprudencia Disposiones</u>
<u>Complementarias, Legislacion de</u>
<u>Seguridad Social para las Fuerzas</u>
<u>Armadas, Ley de Responsabilidades de los</u>
<u>Funcionarios y Empleados Publicos</u>.
Alberto Trueba Urbina y Jorge Trueba
Barrera. 23a ed. Mexico: Editorial
Porrua, 1987.
"Federal Bureaucratic Labor Law:
Commentaries and Jurisprudence
Comlementary Provisiones, Armed Forces
Social Security Legislation, Federal
Civil Servant Responsibility Law."

568. <u>Ley Federal del Trabajo Reformado y</u>
<u>Adicionada: Nuevos Comentarios,</u>
<u>Bibliografia y Jurisprudencia:</u>
<u>Resoluciones de la Comisiones Nacionales</u>
<u>para el Reparto de Utilidades y de</u>
<u>Salario Minimos: Ley del Seguro Social</u>.
Alberto Trueba Urbina y Jorge Trueba
Barrera. 57a ed. Mexico: Editorial
Porrua, 1988.
"Federal Labor Law; Notes,
Jurisprudence, Bibliography, Resolutions
of the National Commission for Profit
Sharing and Minimum Salary, and Social
Security Code."

569. Mexican Labor Law: As of January 10,
     1974, Spanish-English Edition. Chicago:
     Commerce Clearing House, 1974.

570. Tax Laws of the World: Mexico. Alachua,
     Florida: Foreign Tax Association Inc.,
     1981-. Loose-Leaf Service.
     "Federal Labor Code in English."

SECONDARY MATERIAL: SERIALS

571. Barajas Montes de Oca, S. "Lineamientos
     Generales del Amparo en Materia de
     Trabajo." Boletin Mexicano de Derecho
     Comparado 20 (1987): 447-487.
     "General Features of the Writ of
     'Amparo' in Labor Matters."

572. Bartow, Ann M. "The Rights of Workers in
     Mexico (Mexican Labor Law from Three
     Perspectives)." Comparative Labor Law
     Journal 11 (Winter 1990): 182-202.

573. Goldin, Amy H. "Collective Bargaining in
     Mexico: Stifled by the Lack of Democracy
     in Trade Unions (Mexican Labor Law from
     Three Perspectives)." Comparative Labor
     Law Journal 11 (Winter 1990): 203-225.

574. "Mexican Law Symposium: The Claim of
     'Amparo' in Mexico: Constitutional
     Protection of Human Rights. P.P.
     Camargo: The Mexican Notariate. G.F.
     Margadant: Certain Aspects of Mexican
     Labor Laws Especially as They Affect
     Foreign Owned Businesses. R.C.
     Villareal: Administrative Procedures
     Necessary to Secure a Patent in Mexico.
     M. Soni: Private International Law in
     Mexico and the United States: A Brief
     Comparative Study. J.L. Siqueiros."
     California Western Law Review 6 (Spring
     1970): 201-266.

575. Peters, Susanna. "Labor Law for the Maquiladoras: Choosing Between Workers' Rights and Foreign Investment (Mexican Labor Law from Three Perspectives)." Comparative Labor Law Journal 11 (Winter 1990): 226-248.

576. Santos Azuela, H. "El Caracter Procedimental del Derecho de Huelga." Boletin Mexicano de Derecho Comparado 22 (1989): 141-163.
"Procedural Character of the Strike Law."

577. Vega Gomez, Oscar de la. "Settlement of Labor Disputes in Mexico." University of Miami Inter-American Law Review 21 (Fall 1989): 175-183.

578. Ziskind, David and Esther Horney. "Laws Affecting Migratory Labor: United States, Mexico, and Canada." Comparative Labor Law 4 (Winter 1981): 1-25.

SECONDARY MATERIAL: MONOGRAPHS

579. Bailon Valdovinos, Rosalio. Legislacion Laboral. Mexico: Editorial Limusa, 1986.
"Labor Legislation."

580. Barajas, Santiago. Manual de Derecho Administrativo del Trabajo. Mexico: Editorial Porrua, 1985.
"Handbook of Administrative Labor Law."

581. Cueva, Mario de la. Derecho Mexicano del Trabajo. 12a ed. Mexico: Editorial Porrua, 1970.
"Mexican Labor Law."

582. Cueva, Mario de la. <u>El Nuevo Derecho
     Mexicano del Trabajo</u>. 11a ed. Mexico:
     Editorial Porrua, 1988.
     "The New Mexican Labor Laws."

583. Guerrero, Euquerio. <u>Manual de Derecho
     del Trabajo</u>. 16a ed. Mexico: Editorial
     Porrua, 1989.
     "Handbook of Labor Law."

584. Lobato, Jacinto. <u>Nueva Ley Federal del
     Trabajo</u> (Revisada y Actualizada). 16a
     ed. Mexico: Libreria Teocalli, 1986.
     "New Federal Labor Law (Revised and
     Updated)."

585. Munoz, Ramon Roberto. <u>Derecho del
     Trabajo: Teoria General</u>. Mexico:
     Editorial Porrua, 1976.
     "Labor Law: General Theory."

586. Munoz Ramon, Roberto. <u>Derecho del
     Trabajo: Instituciones</u>. Mexico:
     Editorial Porrua, 1983.
     "Labor Law: Institutions."

587. Murg, Gary E. and John C. Fox. <u>Labor
     Relations Law: Canada, Mexico, and
     Western Europe</u>. New York: Practising Law
     Institute, 1978.

588. Pallares, Eduardo. <u>Jurisprudencia de la
     Suprema Corte en Materia Laboral:
     Sintesis y Critica</u>. 2a ed. Mexico:
     Editorial Porrua, 1976.
     "Jurisprudence of the Supreme Court on
     Labor Matters; Synthesis and
     Examination."

589. Porras y Lopez, Armando. <u>Derecho Procesal del Trabajo: De Acuerdo con la Nueva Ley Federal del Trabajo</u>. 3a ed. Mexico: Editorial Porrua, 1975. "Labor Procedural Law; According to the New Federal Labor Law."

590. Santos Azuela, Hector. <u>Estudios de Derecho Sindical y del Trabajo</u>. Mexico: UNAM, 1987. "A Study of Union and Labor Law."

591. Servicio de Informes Sobre Asuntos Laborales. <u>Manual de Acceso a la Jurisprudencia Laboral</u>. Mexico: Secretaria del Trabajo y Prevision Social, 1917-. "Handbook of Labor Jurisprudence."

592. Trueba Urbina, Alberto. <u>Diccionario de Derecho Obrero</u>. 3rd ed. Mexico: Ediciones Botas, 1957. "Dictionary of Labor Law."

593. Trueba Urbina, Alberto y Jorge Trueba Barrera. <u>Ley Federal del Trabajo: Comentarios, Prontuarios, Jurisprudencia y Bibliografia, Salarios Minimos 1986, Nueva Zonas Economicas Salarios, Capacitacion y Adestramiento, Reparto de Utilidades, Ley y Reglamento del INFONAVIT, Reglamento de Trabajo de los Empleados de las Instituciones de Credito y Organizaciones Auxiliares, Reglamento de Seguridad e Higiene</u>. 59a ed. Mexico: Editorial Porrua, 1989. "Federal Labor Law: Commentaries, Compendium of Rules, Jurisprudence and Bibliography, Mininum Wages for 1986,

Mininum Wages for the New Economic
Zones, Training and Teaching, Profits
Sharing, Law and Rules of INFONAVIT,
Regulations of the Work of Employees of
Credit and Related Institutions, Health
Regulations."

Mining Laws

PRIMARY MATERIAL

594. Ley Reglamentaria del Articulo 27
     Constitucional en Materia Minera
     (12-22-75).
     Regulatory Law of Article 27 of the
     Constitution Concerning Mining Matters.

595. Mineria-Disposiones Conexas (2-26-44)
     (12-31-81) 12-31-86).
     Mining-Related Provisions.

596. Reglamento de la Ley Reglamentaria del
     Articulo 27 Constitucional en Materia
     Minera (9-27-90).
     Regulations of the Regulatory Law of
     Article 27 of the Constitution
     Concerning Mining Matters.

597. Reglamento de Seguridad en los Trabajos
     de las Minas (3-13-67).
     Regulations Concerning Mine Safety.

LOCATION OF LEGISLATION

598. Legislacion Minera. 19a ed. Mexico:
     Editorial Porrua, 1988.
     "Mining Legislation."

599. Leyes y Reglamentos Sobre Aguas,
     Bosques, Colonizacion, Minas y Petroleo.
     Mexico: Ediciones Andrade, 1979-.
     Loose-Leaf Service.
     "Laws and Regulations on Water, Forests,
     Colonization, Mines and Oil."

SECONDARY MATERIAL: SERIALS

600. Borek, Theodore B. "Evaluating a
     Developing Institution: Mexicanization
     of Mining." Arizona Law Review 13 (July
     1971): 673-702.

601. Lozano Rocha, Erasmo. "Operating a Mine
     in Mexico--An Overview of the Legal
     Considerations." Rocky Mountain Mineral
     Law Institute Proceedings 27A (1982
     Annual): 553-633.

602. Mainero, C.E. "Legal and Practical
     Aspects of Mexicanization Under the
     Mining Law of Mexico." Rocky Mountain
     Mineral Law Institute 18 (1973):
     595-619.

603. Miranda, Fausto C. "Exploring for
     Minerals in Mexico--An Overview of Legal
     Considerations."
     Rocky Mountain Mineral Law Institute
     Proceedings 27A (Annual 1981): 431-552.

604. Morales Dominguez, A.M. "Political and
     Social Aspects of the Mexican Mining
     Industry." Rocky Mountain Mineral Law
     Institute Proceedings 27A (1982):
     409-429.

605. "Seminar on the Law of Real Property Acquisition in Mexico: Introduction. Investment in Real Property in Mexico: An Overview of Constitutional and Statutory Restrictions. G Gutierrez Quiroz: An Introduction to Secured Real Estate Transactions in Mexico. O. Rivera Farber: The Mexican Land Registry: A Critical Evaluation. B. Kozolchyk: The Mexican Mining Concession--Its Features, Regulation and Practice. G.J. Perez: A Select Bibliography on Mexican Real Property Law. E. Revilla." <u>Arizona Law Review</u> 12 (Summer 1970): 265-389.

SECONDARY MATERIAL: MONOGRAPHS

606. Becerra Gonzalez, Maria. <u>Principios de la Constitucion Mexicana de 1917 Relacionados Con el Subsuelo, Antecedents Tribunales y Legislativos, Principios Fundamentales Contenidos en la Constitucion en su Version Original y Cambios Operados Despues de 1917 en el Mismo Texto Constitucional</u>. Mexico: UNAM, 1967.
"Principles of the Mexican Constitution of 1917 Relating to the Subsoil, Court and Legislative Antecedents, Fundamental Principles Contained in the Constitution in Their Original Form and Changes Made Since 1917 in the Constitutional Text."

607. Berstein, Marvin D. <u>The Mexican Mining Industry, 1890-1950: A Study of the Interaction of Politics, Economic, and Technology</u>. Albany: State University of New York, 1964.

608. Organization of American States, General Secretariat. <u>Mining and Petroleum Legislation: Latin America and the Carribbean</u>. 3rd ed. Dobbs Ferry, New York. Oceana, 1979-. Loose-Leaf Service.

Notary Laws

PRIMARY MATERIAL

609. Arancel del Notario para el Distrito
     Federal (12-31-47) (1-13-86).
     Schedule of Fees for Notaries of the
     Federal District.

610. Ley del Notariado Para el Distrito
     Federal (1-8-80).
     Notary Law of the Federal District.

611. Reglamento del Consejo de Notarios del
     Distrito Federal (2-11-47).
     Regulations of the Commission of
     Notaries of the Federal District.

LOCATION OF LEGISLATION

612. Ley del Notariado para el Distrito
     Federal y Disposiciones Complementarias.
     9a ed. Mexico: Editorial Porrua, 1988.
     "Notary Law of the Federal District and
     Related Legislation."

SECONDARY MATERIAL: SERIALS

613. "Mexican Law Symposium. The Claim of 'Amparo' in Mexico: Constitutional Protection of Human Rights. P.P. Camargo: The Mexican Notariate. G.F. Margadant: Certain Aspects of Mexican Labor Laws Especially as They Affect Foreign Owned Businesses. R.C. Villareal: Administrative Procedures Necessary to Secure a Patent in Mexico. M. Soni: Private International Law in Mexico and the United States: A Brief Comparative Study. J.L. Siqueiros." California Western Law Review 6 (Spring 1970): 201-266.

SECONDARY MATERIAL: MONOGRAPHS

614. Carral y de Teresa, Luis. Derecho Notarial y Derecho Registral. 10a ed. Mexico: Editorial Porrua, 1988. "Notary and Registry Laws."

615. Perez Fernandez del Castillo, Bernardo. Derecho Notarial. 4a ed. Mexico: Editorial Porrua, 1989. "Notary Law."

616. Perez Fernandez del Castillo, Bernardo. Etica Notarial. 2a ed. Mexico: Editorial Porrua, 1986. "Notary Ethics."

617. Perez Fernandez del Castillo, Bernardo. Historia de la Escribania en la Nueva Espana y del Notariado en Mexico. 2a ed. Mexico: Editorial Porrua, 1988. "History of the Office of Clerkship in New Spain and of the Notary in Mexico."

Oil and Gas Laws

PRIMARY MATERIAL

618. Ley del Petroleo (12-31-25).
Oil Law.

619. Ley Reglamentaria del Articulo 27
Constitucional en el Ramo del Petroleo
(11-29-58).
Regulatory Law of Constitutional Article
27 Relating to Oil.

620. Reglamento de la Distribucion de Gas (3-29-60).
Regulations on the Distribution of Gas.

621. Reglamento de la Ley del Petroleo (4-8-26).
Regulations of the Oil Law.

622. Reglamento de la Ley Reglamentaria del
Articulo 27 Constitucional en el Ramo
del Petroleo, para Distribucion de Gas
Licuado. (12-13-50).
Regulatory Law of Constitutional Article
27 Relating to the Oil Law, Concerning
the Distribution of Liquid Gas.

623. Reglamento de Trabajos Petroleros (2-27-74).
     Regulations of Oil Projects.

LOCATION OF LEGISLATION

624. Leyes y Reglamento Sobre Aguas, Bosques,
     Colonizacion, Minas y Petroleo. Mexico:
     Ediciones Andrade, 1937-. Loose-Leaf
     Service
     "Laws and Regulations on Water, Forests,
     Colonization, Mines and Oil."

SECONDARY MATERIAL: SERIALS

625. Joyner, C.C. "Petroleos Mexicanos in a
     Developing Society: The Political
     Economy of Mexico's National Oil
     Industry." George Washington Journal of
     International Law and Economics 17
     (1982): 63-109.

626. "U.S.-Mexico Transboundary Resource
     Issue. Editorial. A.D. Tarlock:
     Introduction to U.S.-Mexico
     Transboundary Resources Issues. W.R.
     Knedlik: Transboundary Resources: A View
     from Mexico. A. Szekely: Hydrocarbons
     Deposits of the Border Region Between
     Mexico and the United States: A
     Preliminary Report. C. Pedrazzini; J.
     Teyssier, Energy on the U.S.-Mexico
     Border. R. Shipman: On an Institutional
     Arrangement for Developing Oil and Gas
     in the Gulf of Mexico. A.E. Utton; P.D.
     McHugh: The International Law of
     Submarine Transboundary Hydrocarbon
     Resources: Legal Limits to Behavior and
     Experiences in the Gulf of Mexico. A.
     Szekey: Conflictual Interdependence:
     United States-Mexican Relations on
     Fishery Resources. B. Cicin-Sain; M.K.
     Orbach; S.J. Sellers; E. Manzanilla:

Transboundary Environmental Problems
Solving: Social Process, Cultural
Perception. The Congress of the United
Mexican States Decrees Federal Act
Relating to the Sea. Transboundary Oil
and Gas Selected Bibliography. A.
Szekey." <u>Natural Resources Journal</u> 26
(Fall 1986): 659-850.

627. Valencia, C.R. "International Sale of
Natural Gas: The Pemex-Border Gas, Inc.
Contract." <u>Texas International Law
Journal</u> Journal 17 (Winter 1982): 15-37.

SECONDARY MATERIAL: MONOGRAPHS

628. Standard Oil Company. <u>The Mexican
Expropriations in International Law</u>. New
Jersey: Standard Oil Company, 1938.

Patent and Trademarks Laws

PRIMARY MATERIAL

629. Ley de Invenciones y Marcas (2-10-76).
Law of Inventions and Trademarks.

630. Reglamento de la Ley de Invenciones y
Marcas (8-30-88).
Regulations of the Law of Inventions and
Trademarks.

631. Reglamento de la Ley Sobre el Control y
Registro de la Transferencia y el Uso y
Explotacion de Patentes y Marcas (1-9-
90).
Regulations of the Law on the Control
and Registration of the Transfer of
Technology and the Use and Exploitation
of Patents and Trademarks.

LOCATION OF LEGISLATION

632. Doing Business in Mexico. Editor Susan
K. Lefler. Albany: Matthew Bender, 1980.
Loose-Leaf Service.
"English Edition of the Law of
Inventions and Trademarks and
Regulations."

633. <u>Legislacion Sobre Propiedad Industrial</u>.
6a ed. Mexico: Ediciones Andrade, 1975.
Loose-Leaf Service.
"Legislation on Industrial Property."

634. <u>Legislacion Sobre Propiedad Industrial,</u>
<u>Transferencia de Tecnologia e</u>
<u>Inversiones Extranjeras</u>. 13a ed. Mexico:
Editorial Porrua, 1988.
"Laws of Industrial Property, Transfer
of Technology and Foreign Investments."

635. "Mexico: Law on the Control and
Registration of the Tranfer of
Technology and the Use and Exploitation
of Patents and Trademarks (English
Translation of Law)." <u>Patent and</u>
<u>Trademark Review</u> 80 (September 1982):
300-307.

636. "Regulation to the Law on the Control
and Registration of the Transfer of
Technology and Exploitation of Patents
and Trademarks (English Translation of
Regulations)." <u>Patent and Trademark</u>
<u>Review</u> 82 (May and June 1982): 225-234
and 274-277.

SECONDARY MATERIAL: SERIALS

637. Barrett, P.J. "Role of Patents in the
Sale of Technology in Mexico." <u>American</u>
<u>Journal of Comparative Law</u> 22 (Spring
1974): 230-280.

638. "Colloquium on Certain Legal Aspects of
Foreign Investments in Mexico:
Regulation of Capital Investment,
Patents and Trademarks, and Transfer of
Technology. Introduction and Initial
Comments. G.M. Wilner: Significant
Innovations of the New Mexican Law on
Inventions and Trademarks. D. Rangel

Medina: Legal Aspects Concerning the Technology Transfer Process in Mexico. J. Alvarez Soberanis: The Law on Foreign Investments. A. Arroija Vizaino." Georgia Journal of International and Comparative Law 7 (Summer 1977): 1-46.

639. Delgado, Jaime. "Patent Litigation Under Mexican Law." Patent and Trademark Review 82 (March 1984): 112-115.

640. Delgado, Jaime. "Patents Working Under Mexican Law." Patent and Trademark Review 78 (November 1980): 443-446.

641. Hyde, Alan L. and Gaston Ramirez de la Corte. "Mexico's 1976 Law of Inventions and Trademarks." Case Western Reserve Journal of International Law 12 (Summer 1980): 469-484.

642. Kransdorf, Geoffrey. "Intellectual Property Trade, and Technology Transfer Law: The United States and Mexico." Boston College Third World Law Journal 7 (Spring 1987): 277-295.

643. "Mexican Law Symposium: The Claim of 'Amparo' in Mexico: Constitutional Protection of Human Rights. P.P. Camargo: The Mexican Notariate. G.F. Margadant: Certain Aspects of Mexican Labor Laws Especially as They Affect Foreign Owned Business. R.C. Villareal: Administrative Procedure Necessary to Secure a Patent in Mexico. M. Soni: Private International Law in Mexico and the United States: a Brief Comparative Study. J.L. Siqueiros." California Western Law Review 6 (Spring 1970): 201-266.

644. "Mexican Law Symposium. The Juridical Regulation of Transnational Enterprises. J.L. Siqueiros: Legal Protection of the Environment in Mexico. L. Cabrera Acevedo: Linking Foreign with Mexican Trademarks: Boon or Bane? D.W. James: Legal Aspects of Activities of Foreign Financial Institutions in Mexico. J.E. Ritch: Defining 'New Lines of Products' Under Mexico's Foreign Investment Law. I. Gomez-Palacio." California Western International Law Journal 8 (Winter 1978): 1-92.

645. "Mexico: Law on the Control and Registration of the Transfer of Technology and the Use and Exploitation of Patents and Trademarks." Patents and Trademark Review 80 (September 1982): 300-307.
"English Excerpts of Laws."

646. "Mexico. U.S.-Mexican Relations: A Need for Mutual Understanding. J. Nava: Mexico: Economic Independence as Basis for Ties to the United States. H.H. Camp: Respect in Friendship. H.B. Margain: Mexico's 1976 Law of Inventions and Trademarks. A.L. Hyde; G. Ramirez de la Corte: U.S.-Mexican Energy Relations in the 1980's: New Resources Versus Old Dilemmas. C.C. Juyner: The U.S.-Mexican Conflict Versus Transboundary Groundwaters: Some Institutional and Political Considerations. S.P. Mumme: Business-Governement Relations in Mexico: The Echeverrian Challenge to the Existing Development Model. E.C. Epstein: Joint Ventures and Technlogy Transfers. B.F. Kryzda." Case Western Law Review 12 (Summer 1980): 449-573.

647. Perez Vargas, J. "Major Innovations Regarding Trade and Service Marks in the Newly Revised Mexican Law on Inventions and Marks--a Mexican Perspective." Trademark Reporter 66 (May-June 1976): 188-204.

648. Rangel, Horacio. "Know-How Licensing in Mexico." Patent and Trademark Review 81 (January 1981): 3-27.

649. Rangel, Horacio. "Las Patentes en Mexico: Evolucion y Sistema." Revista de Investigaciones Juridicas 12 (1988): 241-265.
"Patents in Mexico: Evolution and System."

650. Rangel, Horacio. "Revision of the Mexican Patent Law." International Review of Industrial Property and Copyright 21 (1990): 183-194.

651. Rangel, Horacio. "The Role of Trademarks Use and Registration Under Mexican Law." Patent and Trademark Review 82 (February 1984): 51-62.

652. "Regulations to the Law on the Control and Registration of the Transfer and Exploitation of Patents and Trademarks." Patent and Trademark Review 82 (June 1984): 274-277.

653. Roth, W. "New Law in Mexico: Inventions and Trademarks." The Los Angeles Bar Journal 51 (June 1976): 593-596.

SECONDARY MATERIAL: MONOGRAPHS

654. Alvarez Soberanis, Jaime. <u>La Regulacion de las Invenciones y Marcas y de la Transferencia Tecnologica</u>. Mexico: Editorial Porrua, 1979.
"The Regulations of Inventions and Trademarks and of the Transfer of Technology."

655. Nava Negrete, Justo. <u>Derecho de las Marcas</u>. Mexico: Editorial Porrua, 1985.
"Trademark Law."

656. Seara Vasquez, Modesto. <u>El Sistema Mexicano de Propiedad Industrial: Un Estudio Sobre Patentes, los Certificados de Invencion, las Marcas y la Competencia Desleal</u>. 2a ed. Mexico: Editorial Porrua, 1981.
"The Mexican System of Industrial Property: A Study on Patents, Certificates of Inventions, Trademarks and Unfair Competition."

Political Laws

PRIMARY MATERIAL

657. Ley Federal de Organizaciones Politicas
     y Procesos Electorales (12-30-77).
     Federal Law on Political Organizations
     and the Electral Processes.

658. Ley Organica del Congreso General de los
     Estados Unidos Mexicanos (5-25-79).
     Organic Law of the General Congress of
     the United Mexican States.

659. Reglamento de los Organismos Electorales
     y Provisiones para la Ley Federal de
     Organizaciones Politicas y Procesos
     Electorales (10-27-78).
     Regulations of Electoral Organization
     and Provisiones of the Federal Law of
     Political Organizations and Electoral
     Processes.

LOCATION OF LEGISLATION

660. Codigo Federal Electoral. Mexico:
     Editorial Porrua, 1987.
     "Federal Electoral Code."

661. <u>Ley Federal de Organizaciones Politicas y Procesos Electorales y Su Reglamento</u>. 11a ed. Mexico: Editorial Porrua, 1988. "Federal Law on Political Organizations and the Electoral Processes and Its Regulations."

SECONDARY MATERIAL: SERIALS

662. Monaham, Edward L. "Mexico's Presidential Succession: Miguel de la Madrid and Policy in 1982." <u>Fletcher Forum</u> 6 (Winter 1982): 196-204.

SECONDARY MATERIAL: MONOGRAPHS

663. Andrea Sanchez, Francisco. <u>La Renovacion Politica y el Sistema Electoral Mexicano</u>. Mexico: Editorial Porrua, 1987.
"Political Renewal and the Mexican Electoral System."

664. Cosio Villegas, Daniel. <u>La Sucesion Presidencial</u>. Mexico: Editorial J. Mortiz, 1975.
"Presidential Succession."

665. Lagos Martinez, Silvio. <u>Prontuario de la Ley Organica y del Reglamento para el Gobierno Interior del Congreso General de los Estados Unidos Mexicanos</u>. Mexico: Editorial Porrua, 1983.
"Compendium of the Organic Law and Regulations of the General Congress of the United Mexican States."

666. Molina Pineiro, Luis. Estructura del Poder y Reglas del Juego Politico en Mexico: Ensayo de Sociologia Aplicada. 4a ed. Mexico: UNAM, 1988. "The Structure of Power and the Rules of the Political Game in Mexico: An Essay of Applied Sociology."

667. Morris, Stephen D. Los Presidenciables: Mexico's Next Jefe. Tempe, Arizona: INCAMEX, 1987.

668. Padilla, Remberto H. Historia de la Politica Mexicana: Gobernantes de Mexico. Mexico: Editores Asociados Mexicanos, 1988. "History of Politics in Mexico: Mexican Political Leaders."

Property Laws

PRIMARY MATERIAL

669. Codigo Civil; Libro II (3-26-28).
     Civil Code; Book II.

670. Ley Organica de la Fraccion 1 del
     Articulo 27 de la Constitucion General
     (1-21-26).
     Organic Law of Section 1 of Article 27
     of the General Constitution.

671. Ley Sobre el Regimen de Propiedad en
     Condominio de Inmuebles, para el
     Distrito Federal (12-28-72).
     Law of Condominium Property, for the
     Federal District.

672. Reglamento del Registro Publico de la
     Propiedad (5-6-80).
     Regulations of the Public Registry of
     Property.

LOCATION OF LEGISLATION

673. Codigo Civil para el Distrito Federal.
     56a ed. Mexico: Editorial Porrua, 1988.
     "Civil Code for the Federal District."

674. Codigo Civil para el Distrito Federal en Materia Comun y para Toda la Republica en Materia Federal Comentado. Mexico: Instituto de Investigacion Juridica, Porrua, 1990.
"Civil Code for the Federal District in Ordinary Matters and for the Entire Republic in Federal Matters (Book 2)."

675. Mexican Civil Code. Translated by Michael Wallace Gordon. Dobbs Ferry, New York: Oceana Publications, Inc., 1980.
"English Edition of the Civil Code."

676. Nuevo Codigo Civil para el Distrito Federal en Materia Comun, para Toda la Republica en Materia Federal. Mexico: Ediciones Andrade, 1938-.Loose-Leaf Service.
"New Civil Code for the Federal District in Common Matters, and for All of the Republic in Federal Matters."

SECONDARY MATERIAL: SERIALS

677. Alessio Robles, M. "Derechos Preferenciales en Derecho Mexicano." Revista de Investigaciones Juridicas 11 (1987): 43-81.
"Prior Claim in Mexican Law."

678. Aranda, Luis. "Acquiring Property in Mexico's Forbidden Zones: Estate Planning Considerations." Trusts and Estates 155 (October 1976): 666-669.

679. Diaz y Diaz, M. "Proceso Constitucional y Relaciones de Propiedad: Notas para el Analisis del Caso Mexicano." <u>Revista de Investigaciones Juridicas</u> 11 (1987): 189-251.
"The Constitutional Process and Property: Notes on the Mexican Situtation."

680. Karon, Paul. "Commercial Real Estate Practices and Development in Northwestern Mexico: A Comparative Living Law Description." <u>Arizona Journal of International and Comparative Law</u> 3 (Annual 1984): 10-56.

681. Lopez Monroy, J.J. "El Derecho del Tanto Como Derecho Real." <u>Revista de Investigaciones Juridicas</u> 11 (1987): 319-326.
"Stock Subscription Rights As Rights In Rem."

682. Martinez Guerrero, R. "Acquisition of Real Property, Investment in Corporations and Probate Law in Mexico." <u>Real Property Probate and Trust Journal</u> 10 (Fall 1975): 427-453.

683. "Mexican Law Symposium: The Contemporary Mexican Approach to Growth with Foreign Investment: Controlled but Participatory Independence. M.W. Gordon: The Forbidden Zones in Mexico. V.A. Villaplana: A Constitutional Comparison: Mexico, the United States and Uganda. F.N. Baldwin." <u>California Western Law Review</u> 10 (Fall 1973): 1-104.

684. Ruiz Daza, M. "La Regulacion de Bienes Entre Esposos." Revista de Investigaciones Juridicas 11 (1987): 453-500.
"Regulation of Property Between Spouses."

685. "Seminar on the Law of Real Property Acquisition in Mexico: Introduction. Investment in Real Property in Mexico: An Overview of Constitutional and Statutory Restrictions. G. Gutierrez: An Introduction to Secured Real Estate Transactions in Mexico. O. Rivera Farber: The Mexican Land Registry: A Critical Evaluation. B. Kozolchyk: The Mexican Mining Concession--Its Features, Regulation and Practice. G.J. Perez: A Select Bibliography on Mexican Real Property Law. E. Revilla." Arizona Law Review 12 (Summer 1970): 265-389.

686. "Symposium: Mexican Foreign Investment Laws. Introduction to Recent Developments in Mexican Law: Politics of Modern Nationalism. E.C. Epstein: Mexican Real Estate Transactions by Foreigners. Z.V. Chayet and L.B. Sutton: Land Transfer and Finance in Mexico. M.R. Meek: A Survey of Mexican Laws Affecting Foreign Businessmen. A. Gonzalez-Baz: Transfer of Technology in Mexico. D.H. Brill: Immigration, Importation and Labor Law Applicable to Foreign Businessmen in Mexico. R.L. Tanner: Mexican Taxation: Law and Practice. R.L. Miller: Comment: Mexico's Border Industrial Program: Legal Guidelines for the Foreign Investor." Denver Journal of International Law and Policy 4 (Spring 1974): 1-109.

687. Zanotti, John P. "Mexico's Forbidden
Zones: The Presidential Decree of April
29, 1971." Law and the Social Order
(1973): 455-479.

SECONDARY MATERIAL: MONOGRAPHS

688. Aguilar Carbajal, Leopoldo. Segundo
Curso de Derecho Civil: Bienes, Derecho
Reales y Sucesiones. 4a ed. Mexico:
Editorial Porrua, 1980.
"Second Course of Civil Law: Property,
Federal Taxes and Succession."

689. Colin Sanchez, Guillermo. Procedimiento
Registral de la Propiedad. 2a ed.
Mexico: Editorial Porrua, 1979.
"Registry Procedure for Real Property."

690. Colin Sanchez, Guillermo. Reglamento de
la Prestacion del Servicio Turistico del
Sistema de Tiempo Compartido. Mexico:
Editorial Porrua, 1990.
"Regulations of the Time-Sharing System
for Tourists."

691. Rojina Villegas, Rafael. Derecho Civil
Mexicano. 7a ed. Mexico: Editorial
Porrua, 1987.
"Mexican Civil Law (Covers Property
Rights)."

692. Rojina Villegas, Rafael. Teoria General
de los Derechos Reales. Mexico: (S.N.),
1947.
"General Theory of Jus In Rem."

693. Tancer, Robert S. and John P. Zanotti.
The Mexican Law of Foreign Real Estate
Investment in the Prohibited Zones: An
Overview, 1971-1973. 2nd ed. Tempe:
Center for Latin American Studies,
Arizona State University, 1975.

694. Vallarta, Ignacio Luis. <u>La Propiedad Inmueble por Extranjeros</u>. Mexico: Secretaria de Relaciones Exteriores, 1986.
"Real Estate Ownership by Aliens."

695. Vega, John de la. <u>Mexican Real Estate Law and Practice Affecting Private U.S. Ownership</u>. Tucson, Arizona: University of Arizona, 1974.

Securities and
Stock Market Laws

PRIMARY MATERIAL

696. Ley de Sociedades de Inversion (1-14-85).
Law of Investment Companies.

697. Ley del Mercado de Valores (1-2-75).
Law of the Stock Market.

698. Reglamento de la Bolsa de Valores (2-20-83).
Regulations of the Stock Exchange.

699. Reglas del Registro Nacional de Valores
e Intermediarios (11-22-79).
Rules of the National Registry of
Securities and Intermediaries.

LOCATION OF LEGISLATION

700. Commercial, Business and Trade Laws:
Mexico. Edited and Compiled by Michael
Wallace Gordon. Dobbs Ferry, New York:
Oceana Publications, Inc., 1983-.
Loose-Leaf Service.
"English Edition of the Law of
Commercial Companies."

701. <u>Doing Business in Mexico</u>. Editor Susan K. Lefler. Albany: Matthew Bender, 1980. Loose-Leaf Service.
"English Edition of the Law of the Stock Market."

702. <u>Legislacion Bancaria: Ley General de Instituciones de Credito y Organizaciones Auxiliarias y Disposiciones Complementarias</u>. 32a ed. Mexico: Editorial Porrua, 1988.
"Banking Legislation: General Law of Institutions of Credit and Related Organizations and Complementary Provisions."

703. <u>Legislacion Mercantil</u>. 2a ed. Mexico: Mexico Fiscal y Laboral S.A. de C.V., 1974-. Loose-Leaf Service.
"Commercial Legislation."

704. <u>Legislacion Mercantil y Leyes Conexas: Concordado con los de Alemania, Argentina, Chile, Espana, Francia e Italia</u>. Mexico: Ediciones Adrade, 1974. Loose-Leaf Service.
"Commercial Legislation and Related Laws; Concorded with those of Germany, Argentina, Chile, Spain, France and Italy."

SECONDARY MATERIAL: SERIALS

705. Campo Y Souza, Diego Martin del. "A Public Stock Offering in Mexico." <u>New York University Journal of International Law and Politics</u> 16 (Winter 1984): 305-351.

706. Leon Tovar, S.H. "Decreto Que Reforma, Adiciona y Deroga Disposiciones de La Ley del Mercado de Valores." <u>Boletin Mexicano de Derecho Comparado</u> 21 (1988): 323-329.
     "Decree that Reforms the Stock Market Law."

707. Wolff, Samuel. "A Study of Mexico's Capital Markets and Securities Regulation." <u>Vanderbilt Journal of Transnational Law</u> 20 (August 1987): 385-430.

SECONDARY MATERIAL: MONOGRAPHS

708. Nacional Financiera, S.A. <u>El Mercado de Valores</u>. Mexico: 1971.
     "The Stock Market."

709. Vasquez del Mercado, Oscar. <u>Asambleas, Fusion y Liquidacion de Sociedades Mercantiles</u>. 3a ed. Mexico: Editorial Porrua, 1987.
     "Meetings, Merging and Dissolutions of Commercial Companies."

Social Security Laws

PRIMARY MATERIAL

710. Ley del Instituto de Seguridad Social para las Fuerzas Armadas Mexicanas (6-29-76).
Law of the Institute of Social Security for the Mexican Armed Forces.

711. Ley del Instituto de Seguridad y Servicios Sociales de los Trabajadores del Estado (12-27-83).
Law of the Institute of Social Security for Public Employees.

712. Ley del Seguro Social (3-12-73).
Social Security Law.

713. Reglamento de la Ley del Seguro Social (5-14-43).
Regulations of the Social Security Law.

LOCATION OF LEGISLATION

714. Ley del Seguro Social y Disposiciones Complementarias. 43a ed. Mexico: Editorial Porrua, 1988.
"Social Security Law and Related Provisions."

715. <u>Legislacion Sobre el Trabajo</u>. Mexico: Ediciones Andrade, 1937-. Loose-Leaf Service.
     "Labor Legislation."

716. <u>Tax Laws of the World: Mexico</u>. Alachua, Florida: Foreign Tax Law Association Inc., 1981-. Loose-Leaf Service.
     "English Edition of the Social Security Law."

SECONDARY MATERIAL: SERIALS

717. Ponce de Leon Armenta, L.M. "El Sistema Juridico de la Seguridad Social en Mexico." <u>Boletin Mexicano de Derecho Comparado</u> 21 (1988): 807-817.
     "The Juridical System of Social Security in Mexico."

SECONDARY MATERIAL: MONOGRAPHS

718. Moreno Padilla, Javier. <u>Ley del Seguro Social</u>. 14a ed. Mexico: Editorial Trillas, 1987.
     "Social Security Law."

Tax Laws

PRIMARY MATERIAL

719. Codigo Fiscal de la Federacion
     (12-31-81).
     Tax Code of the Federation.

720. Ley de Coordinacion Fiscal (12-31-87).
     Law of Fiscal Coordination.

721. Ley de Ingresos de la Federacion Para el
     Ejercicio Fiscal de 1987 (12-28-89).
     Income Law of the Federation for the
     Fiscal Year of 1987.

722. Ley del Impuesto al Valor Agregado
     (12-29-78).
     Added Value Tax Law.

723. Ley del Impuesto Especial Sobre
     Produccion y Servicios (12-30-80).
     Special Tax Law on Production and
     Services.

724. Ley del Impuesto Sobre Adquisiciones de
     Inmuebles (12-31-79).
     Real Estate Tax Law.

725. Ley del Impuesto Sobre Automoviles
     Nuevos (12-31-79).
     New Automobile Tax Law.

726. Ley del Impuesto Sobre la Renta
     (12-30-80).
     Income Tax Law.

727. Ley Federal de Derechos (12-31-81).
     Federal Law of Rights.

728. Ley Federal de Impuestos Sobre Herencias
     y Legados (12-30-59).
     Inheritance and Bequest Tax law.

729. Ley Organica del Tribunal Fiscal de la
     Federacion (2-2-78).
     Organic Law of the Tax Court of the
     Federation.

730. Ley Penal de Defraudacion Impositiva en
     Materia Federal (12-31-47).
     Federal Criminal Tax Fraud Law.

731. Reglamento del Codigo Fiscal de la
     Federacion (2-29-84).
     Regulations of the Tax Code of the
     Federation.

LOCATION OF LEGISLATION

732. Codigo Fiscal de la Federacion. 39a ed.
     Mexico: Editorial Porrua, 1988.
     "Tax Code of the Federation."

733. Impuestos del Timbre: Sobre la Renta,
     Ley del Impuesto al Valor Agregado:
     Sucesiones y Donaciones: Codigo Fiscal
     del la Federacion: Con Reglamento y
     Disposiciones Conexas. Mexico: Ediciones
     Andrade, 1931-. Loose-Leaf Service.

"Stamp Tax; Income Tax, Added Value Tax;
Successions and Donations, Tax Code;
with Related Provisiones."

734. Impuestos Sobre la Renta. 10a ed.
Mexico: Editorial Fiscal y Laboral, S.A.
de C.V., 1976-. Loose-Leaf Service.
"Income Tax Law."

735. Ley del Impuesto al Valor Agregado y Su
Reglamento. 11a ed. Mexico: Editorial
Porrua, 1988.
"Added Value Tax Law and Its
Regulations."

736. Ley del Impuesto Sobre la Renta:
Reglamento y Disposiciones
Complementarias. 46a ed. Mexico:
Editorial Porrua, 1988.
"Income Tax Law: And Related
Provisions."

737. Mexican Income and Commercial Receipt
Tax Laws, as of January 1. 1977.
Chicago: Commerce Clearing House, 1977.

738. Tax Laws of the World: Mexico. Alachua,
Florida: Foreign Tax Law Association,
Inc., 1981-. Loose-Leaf Service.
"English Edition of All of the Major Tax
Legislation."

SECONDARY MATERIAL: SERIALS

739. Aguirre, Carlos A. and Parthasarati
Shome. "The Mexican Value-Added Tax
(VAT): Methodology for Calculating the
Base." National Tax Journal 41 (December
1988): 543-554.

740. Calvo Nicolau, Enrique. "Mexican Taxes on Foreign Investment and Trade (The New Environment for Trade and Investment in Mexico)." Houston Journal of International Law 12 (Spring 1990): 265-290.

741. Engle, Howard S. "Mexican Tax Reform." Journal of Corporate Taxation 16 (Winter 1990): 396-397.

742. Falcone, A.C. "Mexico's In-Bond Manufacturing Program: U.S. Tax Considerations After the 1986 Tax Act." Taxes 65 (April 1987): 211-220.

743. Jenkins, Glenn P. "The Taxation of Foreign Investment Income in Canada, the United States and Mexico." Law and Contemporary Problems 44 (Summer 1981): 143-159.

744. Karlin, Michael and Paula E. Breger. "Mexico and U.S. Exchange Tax Information: Mexico Hopes to Curb Flight of Capital." Los Angeles Lawyer 13 (November 1990): 15-19.

745. Klein, James P. "Mexican Taxation of Employee Benefits." International Tax Journal 10 (November 1983): 33-40.

746. Jimenez Illescas, J.M. "Algunas Consideraciones Sobre la Regulacion Fiscal del Fideicomiso en Mexico." Revista de Investigaciones Juridicas 11 (1987):285-303.
"Some Thoughts on Tax Regulations Concerning Trusts in Mexico."

747. Marti, Mary Mercedes. "Survey of Changing Attitudes in Latin American Tax Policy." International Tax Journal 8 (December 1981): 115-131.

748. "Possible Tax Deferral for Interest on Mexican Private Sector Loans." International Tax Journal 9 (May 1983): 286-287.

749. Smith, William J.A. "Effective Tax Planning for Mexican Operations." Oil and Gas Tax Quarterly 29 (June 1981): 685-693.

750. "Symposium: Mexican Foreign Investment Laws. Introduction to Recent Developments in Mexican Law: Politics of Modern Nationalism. E.C. Epstein: Mexican Real Estate Transactions by Foreigners. Z.V. Chayet; L.V.B. Sutton: Land Transfer and Finance in Mexico. M.R. Meek: A Study of Mexican Laws Affecting Foreign Businessmen. A. Gonzales-Baz: Transfer of Technology, Importation and Labor Law Applicable to Foreign Businessmen in Mexico. R.L. Tanner: Mexican Taxation: Law and Practice. R.L.V. Miller: Comment: Mexico's Border Industrial Program: Legal Guidelines for the Foreign Investor." Denver Journal of International Law and Policy 4 (Spring 1974): 1-109.

SECONDARY MATERIAL: MONOGRAPHS

751. Cervantes Montenegro, Joaquin. El Cumplimiento de las Sentencias que Emit el Tribunal Fiscal de la Federacion. Mexico: UNAM, 1988.
"The Enforcement of Verdicts Rendered by the Tax Court of the Federation."

752. The Foreign and the Mexican Tax System.
Prepared by the Income Undersecretary
and the Income Technical General
Direction. [s.l.]: Editorial Porrua,
1986.

753. Garcia Dominguez, Miguel Angel. Teoria
de la Infraccion Fiscal: Derecho Fiscal-
Penal. Mexico: Editorial Cardenas, 1982.
"Theory of the Tax Violation: Criminal
Tax Law."

754. Garza, Sergio Francisco de la. Evolucion
de los Conceptos de Renta y de Ganacias
de Capital en la Doctrina y en la
Legislacion Mexicana Durante el Periodo
de 1921-1980. Mexico: Tribunal Fiscal de
la Federacion, 1983.
"Evolution of the Concepts of Income and
Capital Gains in the Doctrine and
Legislation of Mexico During the Period
of 1921-1980."

755. LegIforme: Informacion al Dia Sobre
Renta. Mexico: Editorial Fiscal y
Laboral, S.A. de C.V., 1982-, (Monthly).
"Up-To-Date Tax Information."

756. Mendoza Vera, Blanca Alicia. La
Jurisprudencia del Tribunal Fiscal de la
Federacion y el Recurso de Queja.
Mexico: UNAM, 1985.
"Jurisprudence of the Tax Court of the
Federation and the Appeals Process."

757. Porras y Lopez, Armando. Derecho Fiscal:
Aspectos Juridcos-Contables. 3a ed.
Mexico: Textos Universitarios, 1972.
"Tax Law: Legal Bookkeeping Aspects."

758. Porras y Lopez, Armando. Derecho
     Procesal Fiscal: Doctrina, Legislacion y
     Jurisprudencia. 2a ed. Mexico: Textos
     Universitarios, 1974.
     "Procedural Tax Law: Doctrine,
     Legislation, and Jurisprudence."

759. Rivera Silva, Manuel. Derecho Penal
     Fiscal. Mexico: Editorial Porrua, 1984.
     "Criminal Tax Law."

760. Sanchez Martinez, Francisco. Formulario
     de Fiscal y Jurisprudencia. 2a ed.
     Mexico: Editorial Porrua, 1986.
     "Tax Formulary and Jurisprudence."

761. Treasury Undersecretary and the Income
     Technical General Direction. The Foreign
     and the Mexican Tax System. Mexico:
     1986.

762. Treasury Undersecretary and the Income
     Technical General Direction. The Fiscal
     Reform for 1987. Mexico: 1986.

763. Tribunal Fiscal de la Federacion:
     Cuarenta y Cinco Anos al Servicio de
     Mexico. Mexico: El Tribunal, 1987-1988.
     "Tax Court of the Federation: Forty-five
     Years at the Service of Mexico."

Torts Laws

PRIMARY MATERIAL

764. Codigo Civil; Libro 4, Capitulo 5 (3-26-28).
Civil Code; Book 4, Chapter 5.

LOCATION OF LEGISLATION

765. <u>Codigo Civil para el Distrito Federal</u>.
57a ed. Mexico: Editorial Porrua, 1988.
"Civil Code for the Federal District."

766. <u>Doing Business in Mexico</u>. Editor Susan
K. Lefler. Albany: Matthew Bender, 1980.
Loose-Leaf Service.
"English Edition of the Tort Articles."

767. <u>Mexican Civil Code</u>. Translated by
Michael Wallace Gordon. Dobbs Ferry, New
York: Oceana Publications, Inc., 1980.
"English Edition of the Civil Code."

768. <u>Nuevo Codigo Civil para el Distrito
Federal en Materia Comun, y para Toda la
Republica en Materia Federal</u>. Mexico:
Ediciones Andrade, 1938-. Loose-Leaf
Service.

"New Civil Code for the Federal District in Ordinary Matters, and for All of the Republic in Federal Matters."

SECONDARY MATERIAL: SERIALS

769. Butte, W.L. "Strict Liability in Mexico." <u>American Journal of Comparative Law</u> 8 (Summer 1970): 805-830.

770. Friedler, E. "Moral Damages in Mexican Law: A Comparative Approach." <u>Loyola of Los Angeles International and Comparative Law Journal</u> 8 (1986): 235-275.

771. Kozolchyk, Boris. "Mexican Law of Damages for Automobile Accidents: Damages or Restitution?" <u>Arizona Journal of International and Comparative Law</u> 1 (Winter 1982): 189-212.

772. "Texas Dissimilarity Doctrine as Applied to the Tort Law of Mexico: A Modern Evaluation." <u>Texas Law Review</u> 55 (August 1977): 1281-1305.

SECONDARY SOURCES: MONOGRAPHS

None

Tourism Laws

PRIMARY MATERIAL

773. Ley Federal de Fomento al Turismo (1-
     28-74).
     Federal Law for the Promotion Tourism.

774. Ley Federal de Turimso (2-6-84).
     Federal Tourism Law.

775. Reglamento de las Agencias de Viaje (10-
     10-69).
     Regulations for Travel Agencies.

LOCATION OF LEGISLATION

776. <u>Extranjeria: Turismo y Poblacion:
     Contiene Ademas Ley Federal de
     Estadisticas y Su Reglamento Asi Como
     Disposiciones Conexas</u>. Mexico: Ediciones
     Andrade, 1962-. Loose-Leaf Service.
     "Alienage; Tourism and Population: Also
     Contains the Federal Law of Statistics
     and Its Regulations as Well as Related
     Provisions."

777. <u>Ley Federal de Turismo</u>. 2a ed. Mexico:
     Editorial Porrua, 1988.
     "Federal Tourism Law."

778. Ley Federal de Turismo y Reglamento.
     Mexico: Interior de la Secretaria de
     Turismo. Publicaciones Administrativas y
     Contables, S.A., 1982.
     "Federal Tourism Law and Regulations."

SECONDARY MATERIAL: SERIALS

779. Tancer, R.S. "Tourist Promotion in
     Mexico." Law and the Social Order
     (Summer 1972): 559-579.

SECONDARY MATERIAL: MONOGRAPHS

780. Colin Sanchez, Guillermo. Reglamento de
     la Prestacion del Servicio Turistico del
     Sistema de Tiempo Compartido. Mexico:
     Editorial Porrua, 1990.
     "Regulations of Time-Sharing
     Accomodations for Tourists."

781. Olivera Toros, Jorge. Legislacion y
     Organizacion Turistica Mexican. 3a ed.
     Mexico: Editorial Porrua, 1988.
     "Legislation and Organization of Mexican
     Tourism."

782. Vallarta, Ignacio Luis. La Propiedad
     Inmueble por Extranjeros. Mexico:
     Secretaria de Relaciones Exteriores,
     1986.
     "Real Estate Ownership by Aliens."

Transfer of
Technology Laws

PRIMARY MATERIAL

783. Ley Sobre el Control y Registro de la
     Transferencia de Tecnologia y el Uso y
     Explotacion de Patentes y Marcas
     (1-11-82).
     Law on the Control and Registration of
     the Transfer of Technology and Use and
     Exploitation of Trademarks and Patents.

784. Reglamento de la Lay Sobre el Control y
     Registro de la Transferencia de
     Tecnology y el Uso y Explotacion de
     Patentes y Marcas (11-25-82).
     Regulations of the Law on the Control
     and Registry of the Transfer of
     Technology and Use and Exploitation of
     Trademarks and Patents.

LOCATION OF LEGISLATION

785. <u>Doing Business in Mexico</u>. Editor Susan
     K. Lefler. Albany: Matthew Bender, 1980.
     Loose-Leaf Service.
     "English Edition of the Law of
     Technology Transfer and the Use and
     Exploitation of Patents and Trademarks."

786. <u>Legislacion Sobre Propiedad Industrial,
Transferencia de Tecnologia e
Inversiones Extranjeras</u>. 13a ed. Mexico:
Editorial Porrua, 1988.
"Legislation on Industrial Property,
Transfer of Technology and Foreign
Investments."

787. "Mexico: Law on the Control and
Registration of the Transfer of
Technology and the Use and Exploitation
of Patents and Trademarks." <u>Patent and
Trademarks Review</u> 80 (September 1982):
300-307.
"English Edition of the Regulations."

788. "Regulations to the Law on the Control
and Registration of the Transfer of
Technology and Exploitation of Patents
and Trademarks." <u>Patent and Trademark
Review</u> 82 (May and June 1984): 225-234
and 274-277.
"English Edition of the Regulations."

789. <u>Tax Laws of the World: Mexico</u>. Alachua,
Florida: Foreign Tax law Association,
Inc., 1981-. Loose-Leaf Service.
"English Edition of the Transfer of
Technology Law."

SECONDARY MATERIAL: SERIALS

790. Camp, H.H. "Recent Developments Under
the Mexican Foreign Investment Law and
the Law Regulating the Transfer of
Technology." <u>Lawyer of the Americas</u> 8
(Fall 1976): 1-35.

791. "Colloquium on Certain Legal Aspects of Foreign Investments in Mexico: Regulation of Capital Investment, Patents and Trademarks, and Transfer of Technology. Introduction and Initial Comments. G.M. Wilner: Significant Innovations of the New Mexican Law on Inventions and Trademarks. D. Rangel Medina: Legal Aspects Concerning the Technology Transfer Process in Mexico." Georgia Journal of International and Comparative Law 7 (Summer 1977):1-46.

792. Delgado, Jaime. "Mexico: Commentary on the Amended Technology Law." Patent and Trademark Review 80 (September 1982): 295-299.

793. Hollman, S.N. "Mexican Restrictions on Foreign Investment and Technology." The Practical Lawyer 20 (Fall 1974): 55-60.

794. Hyde, Alan L. "1981 Mexican Transfer of Technology Law." Lawyer of the Americas 15 (Spring 1983): 37-45.

795. Hyde, A.L. "Mexico's New Transfer of Technology and Foreign Investment Laws: To What Extent Have the Rules Changed?" International Lawyer 10 (Spring 1976): 231-252.

796. Kransdorf, Geoffrey. "Intellectual Property Trade, and Technology Transfer Law: The United States and Mexico." Boston College Third World Law Journal 7 (Spring 1987): 277-295.

797. Kryzda, Bill F. "Joint Ventures and Technology Transfers." Case Western Reserve Journal of International Law 12 (Summer 1980): 549-573.

798. "Mexico: Law on the Control and Registration of the Transfer of Technology and the Use and Exploitation of Patents and Trademarks." Patent and Trademark Review 80 (September 1982):300-307.
"English Edition of Laws."

799. "Mexico. U.S.-Mexican Relations: A Need for Mutual Understanding. J. Nava: Mexico: Economic Independence as Basis for Ties to the United States. H.H. Camp: Respect in Friendship. H.B. Margain: Mexico's 1976 Law of Inventions and Trademarks. A.L. Hyde, G. Ramirez de la Corte: U.S.-Mexican Energy Relations in the 1980's: New Resources Versus Old Dilemmas. C.C. Joyner: The U.S.-Mexican Conflict Over Transboundary Groundwaters: Some Institutional and Political Considerations. S.P. Mumme: Business-Government Relations in Mexico: The Echeverrian Challenge to the Existing Development Model. E.C. Epstein: Joint Ventures and Technology Transfer. B.F. Kryzda." Case Western Reserve Journal of International Law 12 (Summer 1980): 449-573.

800. "Regulations to the Law on the Control and Registration of the Transfer and Exploitation of Patents and Trademarks." Patent and Trademark Review 82 (June 1985): 274-277.

801. "Symposium: Mexican Foreign Investment Laws. Introduction to Recent Developments In Mexican Law: Politics of Modern Nationalism. E.C. Epstein: Mexican Real Estate Transactions by Foreigners. Z.V. Chayet, L.V.B. Sutton: Land Transfer and Finance in Mexico. M.R. Meek: A Survey of Mexican Laws

Affecting Businessmen. A. Gonzalez-Baz:
Transfer of Technology in Mexico. D.H.
Brill: Immigration, Importation and
Labor Law Applicable to Foreign
Businessmen in Mexico. R.L. Tanner:
Mexican Taxation: Law and Practice.
R.L.V. Miller: Comments: Mexico's Border
Industrial Program: Legal Guidelines for
the Foreign Investor." Denver Journal of
International Law and Policy 4 (Spring
1974): 1-109.

SECONDARY MATERIAL: MONOGRAPHS

802. Alvarez Soberanis, Jaime. La Regulacion
de las Invenciones y Marcas y de la
Transferencia Tecnologica. Mexico:
Editorial Porrua, 1979.
"The Regulation of Inventions and
Trademarks and the Transfer of
Technology."

803. Legal Aspects of Doing Business in Latin
America: Mexico, Brazil, Argentina,
Chile, and the Andean Common Market
Countries. New York: Practising Law
Institute, 1980.

804. Perez Miranda, Rafael and Fernando
Serrano Migallon. Tecnologia y Derecho
Economico: Regimen Juridico de la
Apropiacion y Transferencia de
Tecnologia. Mexico: M.A. Porrua, 1983.
"Technology and Economic Law: Legal
Framework for Appropriation and Transfer
of Technology."

805. Technology Transfer: Laws and Practice
in Latin America. Edited by Beverly May
Carl. Revised edition, Chicago:
American Bar Association, 1980.

806. Whiting, Van R. <u>The Politics of Technology Transfer in Mexico</u>. La Jolla, California: University of California, San Diego, 1984.

Transportation Laws

PRIMARY MATERIAL

807. Ley de Navegacion y Comercio Maritimos
(11-21-63).
Law of Navigation and Maritime Commerce.

808. Ley de Vias Generales de Comunicacion
(2-19-40).
Law of General Means of Communications.

809. Ley del Impuesto Sobre Tenecia o Uso de
Vehiculos (12-30-80).
Tax Law on Vehicle Ownership or Use of
Vehicles.

810. Ley del Registro Federal de Vehiculos
(12-30-77).
Law of the Federal Registry of Vehicles.

811. Ley Organica de los Ferrocarriles
Nacionales de Mexico (1-14-85).
Organic Law of the National Railroads of
Mexico.

812. Ley Sobre Construccion de Caminos en
Cooperacion Con los Estados (5-8-34).
Law on Highway Construction with the
Cooperation of the States.

LOCATION OF LEGISLATION

813. <u>Ley de Vias Generales de Comunicacion</u>.
     17a ed. Mexico: Editorial Porrua, 1988.
     "Law of General Means of
     Communications."

814. <u>Leyes y Reglamentos Sobre Comunicaciones</u>
     <u>y Transportes: Contiene, Ademas, las</u>
     <u>Disposiciones Expedidas en Materia de</u>
     <u>Comunicaciones Terrestres, por Agua,</u>
     <u>Aereas, Electricas y Postales</u>. Mexico:
     Ediciones Andrade, 1943-. Loose-Leaf
     Service.
     "Laws and Regulations on Communications
     and Transport; Also Contains Legislation
     Relating to Communications by Land,
     Water, Air, Electrical, and Postal."

SECONDARY MATERIAL: SERIALS

None

SECONDARY MATERIAL: MONOGRAPHS

None

Trust Laws

PRIMARY MATERIAL

815. Ley General de Titulos y Operaciones de
     Credito; Capitulo 5, Articulos 346-359
     (8-27-32).
     General Law of Securities and Credit
     Operations; Chapter 5, Articles 346-359.

LOCATION OF LEGISLATION

816. Codigo de Comercio y Leyes
     Complementarias. 45a ed. Mexico:
     Editorial Porrua, 1988.
     "Commercial Code and Complementary
     Provisions."

817. Legislacion Mercantil. 2a ed Mexico:
     Mexico Fiscal y Laboral, S.A. de C.V.
     1974-. Loose-Leaf Service.
     "Commercial Legislation."

818. Legislacion Mercantil y Leyes Conexas:
     Concordado con los de Alemania,
     Argentina, Chile, Espana, Francia e
     Italia. Mexico: Ediciones Andrade, 1974.
     Loose-Leaf Service.

"Commercial Legislation and Related
Laws; Concorded with those of Germany,
Argentina, Chile, Spain, France and
Italy."

819. Ley General de Titulos y Operaciones de
Credito. 33a ed. Mexico: Editorial
Porrua, 1988.
"General Law of Securities and Credit
Operations."

SECONDARY MATERIAL: SERIALS

820. Diaz Rivera, E.I. "Las Casas de Bolsa en
la Actividad Fiduciaria." Revista de la
Facultad de Derecho de Mexico. 34
(1984): 723-727.
"The Stock Exchange in Trust
Activities."

SECONDARY MATERIAL: MONOGRAPHS

821. Batiza, Rodolfo. El Fideicomiso: Teoria
y Practica. 4 ed. Mexico: Editorial
Porrua, 1980.
"The Trust: Theory and Practice."

822. Batiza, Rodolfo. Principios Basicos del
Fideicomiso y de la Administracion
Fiduciaria. 2a ed. Mexico: Editorial
Porrua, 1985.
"Basic Principles of the Trust and of
the Fiduciary Administration."

823. Dominguez Martinez, Jorge Alfredo. El
Fideicomiso Ante la Teoria General del
Negocio Juridico. 3a ed. Mexico:
Editorial Porrua, 1982.
"The Trust Before the General Theory of
the Juristic Act."

824. Lepaulle, Pierce George. _Tratado Teorico y Practica de los Trusts en Derecho Interno, en Derecho Fiscal y en Derecho Internacional: Seguido de Tres Articulos Sobre el Mismo Tema_. Mexico: Editorial Porrua, 1975.
"Theoretical Study of the Trust in Internal Legislation and in Tax Law and International Law; Followed by Three Other Essays on the Same Subject."

825. Munoz, Luis. _El Fideicomiso_. 2a ed. Mexico: Cardenas, 1980.
"The Trust."

826. Villagorda Lozano, Jose Manuel. _Doctrina General del Fideicomiso_. 2a ed. Mexico: Editorial Porrua, 1982.
"General Doctrine of the Trust."

Water Laws

PRIMARY MATERIAL

827. Ley de Conservacion del Suelo y Agua
(7-6-46).
Soil and Water Conservation Law.

828. Ley Federal de Aguas (1-11-72).
Federal Water Law.

829. Ley Federal del Mar (1-8-86).
Federal Law of the Sea.

830. Reglamento de la Ley de Aguas de
Propiedad Nacional (4-21-36).
Regulations of the Law of Water
Belonging to the State.

831. Reglamento del Articulo 124 de la Ley
Federal de Aguas (12-3-75).
Regulations of Article 124 of the
Federal Water Law.

LOCATION OF LEGISLATION

832. Ley Federal de Aguas. 13a ed. Mexico:
Editorial Porrua, 1988.
"Federal Water Law."

833. <u>Leyes y Reglamentos Sobre Aguas,
     Bosques, Colonizacion, Minas y Petroleo</u>.
     Mexico: Ediciones Andrade, 1937-.
     Loose-Leaf Service.
     "Laws and Regulations on Water, Forests,
     Colonization, Mines and Oil."

SECONDARY MATERIAL: SERIALS

834. Gross, Jeffery. "Transboundary Water
     Quantity: The Effect of Arizona and
     Mexican Groundwater Law on Arizona's
     Agriculture." <u>Arizona Journal of
     International and Comparative Law</u>
     (Annual 1988): 189-199.

835. Mumme, Stephen P. and Scott T. Moore.
     "Agency Autonomy in Transboundary
     Resource Management: The United States
     Section of the International Boundary
     and Water Commission, United States and
     Mexico." <u>Natural Resources Journal</u> 30
     (Summer 1990): 661-684.

836. Oyarzabal, Francisco. "Comentarios a las
     Leyes e Instituciones Que Reglamentan
     las Aguas Superficiales de Mexico."
     <u>Natural Resources Journal</u> 22 (October
     1982): 999-1005.
     "Commentaries on the Laws and
     Institutions That Regulate Above-Ground
     Water."

837. Palacios Velez, Oscar, [et al.]. "En
     Balance de Sales del Distrito de Riego
     de Mexicali." <u>Natural Resources Journal</u>
     18 (January 1978): 49-67.
     "Salt Balances in the Mexicali
     Irrigation District."

SECONDARY MATERIAL: MONOGRAPHS

838. Chavez P. De Velazquez, Martha. Ley
     Federal de Aguas (1972): Exposicion de
     Motivos, Transcripciones para Su
     Interpretacion Autentica, Antecedents
     Legislativos, Correlaciones y
     Jurisprudencia. 2a ed. Mexico: Editorial
     Porrua, 1979.
     "Federal Water Law (1972): Legislative
     History and Jurisprudence."

Miscellaneous

DICTIONARIES

839. <u>Diccionario Fundamental del Espanol de
     Mexico</u>. Mexico: Comision Nacional Para
     la Defensa del Idioma Espanol. El
     Colegio de Mexico: Fondo de Cultura
     Economica, 1982.
     "Fundamental Dictionary of the Spanish
     of Mexico."

840. Instituto de Investigaciones Juridicas.
     <u>Diccionario Juridico Mexicano</u>. 2a ed.
     Mexico: Editorial Porrua, 1988.
     "Mexican Legal Dictionary."

841. Rivera Garcia, Ignacio. <u>Diccionario de
     Terminos Juridicos</u>. 2a ed. Oxford, New
     Hampshire: Equity Publishing Company,
     1985.
     "Dictionary of Juridical Terms."

842. Robb, John A. <u>Dictionary of Legal Terms:
     Spanish-English and English-Spanish</u>.
     16th ed. New York: Wiley and Sons, Inc.,
     1988.

843. Pina, Rafael de. <u>Diccionario de Derecho</u>.
     15a ed. Mexico: Editorial Porrua, 1988.
     "Dictionary of Law."

JURISPRUDENCE AND THE SUPREME COURT

844. Boletin de Informacion Juridica. Mexico:
     Mayo Ediciones, 1945-.
     "Bulletin of Juridical Information
     (Supreme Court Reports)."

845. Castro Zavaleta, Salvador. 55 Anos de
     Jurisprudencia Mexicana. Mexico:
     Cardenas, 1976.
     "55 Years of Mexican Jurisprudence."

846. Guerrero Lara, Ezquiel. La
     Interpretacion Constitucional de la
     Suprema Corte de Justicia (1917-1984).
     2a ed. Mexico: Instituto de
     Investigaciones Juridicas, UNAM, 1985.
     "The Constitutional Interpretation of
     the Supreme Court 1917-1984."

847. Guerrero Lara, Ezequiel. Manual para el
     Manejo del Semanario Judicial de la
     Federacion. Mexico: UNAM, 1982.
     "How to Research in the Judicial Weekly
     of the Federation."

848. Informe. Mexico: Mayo Ediciones, 1927-.
     "Report (Annual Report of the Supreme
     Court)."

849. Manual de Acceso a la Jurisprudencia
     Laboral. Mexico: Secretaria del Trabajo
     y Prevision Social, 1917-.
     "Handbook on Labor Jurisprudence."

850. Pallares, Eduardo. Formulario de Juicios
     Civiles. 17a ed. Mexico: Editorial
     Porrua, 1989.
     "Formulary of Civil Law Cases."

851. Pallares, Eduardo. Formulario y
     Jurisprudencia de Juicios Mercantiles.
     9a ed. Mexico: Editorial Porrua, 1985.
     "Formulary and Jurisprudence of
     Commercial Law Cases."

852. Pallares, Eduardo. Jurisprudencia de la
     Suprema Corte en Materia Laboral:
     Sintesis y Critica. 2a ed. Mexico:
     Editorial Porrua, 1976.
     "Jurisprudence of the Supreme Court on
     Labor Matters: Synthesis and
     Examination."

853. Sanchez Martinez, Francisco. Formulario
     de Fiscal y Jurisprudencia. 2a ed.
     Mexico: Editorial Porrua, 1986.
     "Tax Formulary and Jurisprudence."

854. Sanchez Martinez, Francisco. Formulario
     del Juicio de Amparo y Jurisprudencia.
     5a ed. Mexico: Editorial Porrua, 1986.
     "Formulary of the Writ of `Amparo' and
     Jurisprudence."

855. Selected Mexican Cases. Edited by
     Woodfin L. Butte. Austin: University of
     Texas, School of Law, 1970.

856. Semanario Judicial de la Federacion.
     Mexico: Mayo Ediciones, 1871-.
     "Juridical Weekly of the Federation
     (Supreme Court Reports)."

857. Tellez Ulloa, Marco Antonio.
     Jurisprudencia Mercantil Mejicana. (s.
     n.), 1983.
     "Mexican Commercial Jurisprudence."

858. Tellez Ulloa, Marco Antonio.
     <u>Jurisprudencia Sobre Titulos y
     Operaciones de Credito: La Ley de
     Titulos y Operaciones de Credito Con
     Jurisprudencia y Ejecutorias en su
     Articulado.</u> 2a ed. Hermosillo, Mexico:
     Editorial del Carmen, 1980.
     "Jurisprudence on Securities and Credit
     Operations: The Law and Jurisprudence
     with Decisiones Arranged by Article."

859. <u>Tesis y Jurisprudencia Sobresaliente</u>.
     Mexico: Mayo Ediciones, 1917-.
     "Cases of Note and Jurisprudence
     (Supreme Court Reports)."

860. Trueba Urbina, Alberto y Jorge Trueba
     Barrera. <u>Nueva Legislacion de Amparo
     Reformada: Doctrina, Textos y
     Jurisprudencia</u>. 52a ed. Mexico:
     Editorial Porrua, 1990.
     "New Legislation on the Writ of
     'Amparo': Doctrine, Texts and
     Jurisprudence."

LEGAL HISTORY

861. Batiza, Rodolfo. <u>Las Fuentes del Codigo
     Civil de 1928: Introduccion, Notas y
     Textos de Sus Fuentes Originales No
     Reveladas</u>. Mexico: Editorial Porrua,
     1979.
     "Origins of the 1928 Civil Code:
     Introduction, Notes and Text of Original
     Sources Not Revealed Before."

862. <u>Derecho Publico Mexicanos: Compilacion
     Que Contiene: Importantes Documentos
     Relativos a la Independencia, la
     Constitutcion de Apztzingan, el Plan de
     Iguala, Tratados de Cordoba, la Acta de
     Independencia, Cuestiones de Derecho
     Publico Resueltas por la Soberana Junta</u>

Gubernativa, Cuestiones Constitucionales
Tratados por el Primer Congreso
Constituyente. Mexico: Imprenta del
Gobierno, 1871.
"Constitutions and Other Important
Documents of Mexican Legal History."

863. Esquivel Obregon, Toribio. Apuntes para
la Historia del Derecho en Mexico. 2a
ed. Mexico: Editorial Porrua, 1984.
"Annotations on the Legal History of
Mexico."

864. Gonzalez, Maria del Refugio. Estudios
Sobre la Historia del Derecho Civil en
Mexico Durante el Siglo XIX. Mexico:
UNAM, 1981.
"A Study of the History of Civil Law in
Mexico During the 19th Century."

865. Margadant S., Guillermo Flores.
Introduction to the History of Mexican
Law. Dobbs Ferry, New York: Oceana
Publications, Inc., 1983.

866. Moto Salazar, Efran. Elementos de
Derecho. 31a ed. Mexico: Editorial
Porrua, 1985.
"Elements of Law."

LEGISLATIVE NEWS

867. Alerta de Legislacion Nacional. Mexico:
Instituto de Investigaciones Juridicas,
Centro de Informacion de Legislacion y
Jurisprudencia, 1984.
"Alert of National Legislation (Ceased
Publication in 1984)."

868. Anuario Juridico. Mexico: Instituto de
Investigaciones Juridicas, UNAM.1974-.
"Juridical Annual."

869. Repertorio Anual de Legislacion Nacional
y Extranjera. Mexico: Instituto de
Derecho Comparado, UNAM, 1958-1967.
(Continued by Next Entry).
"Annual Digest of National and Foreign
Legislation."

870. Repertorio Anual de Legislacion
Nacional. Mexico: Instituto de
Investigaciones Juridicas, UNAM,
1968-1971. (Continued by Next Entry).
"Annual Digest of National Legislation."

871. Legislacion y Jurisprudencia. Mexico:
Instituto de Investigaciones Juridicas,
UNAM. 1972-1985. (Continued by Next
Entry).
"Legislation and Jurisprudence."

872. Gaceta Informative de Legislacion
Nacional. Mexico: Instituto de
Investigaciones Juridicas, UNAM. 1985-.
"Informative Gazette of National
Legislation."

873. Boletin del Instituto de Derecho
Comparado de Mexico. Mexico: UNAM.
1948-1967. (Continued by Next Entry).
"Bulletin of the Institute of
Comparative Studies of Mexico."

874. Boletin Mexicano de Derecho Comparado de
Mexico, Nueva Serie. Mexico: Instituto
de Investigaciones Juridicas, UNAM.
1968-.
"Mexican Bulletin of Comparative Law."

875. Business Mexico: A Comprehensive,
Authoritative Look at Today's Mexico,
and Its Economic, Investment and Trade
Prospects. Mexico: American Chamber of
Commerce of Mexico, Monthly.

PRACTICE ORIENTED BOOKS

876. Almada, Carlos F. [et al.]. <u>Derecho Federal Mexicano</u>. Mexico: Editorial Porrua, 1984.
"Mexican Federal Law."

877. Arellano Garcia, Carlos. <u>Practica Juridica</u>. 2a ed. Mexico: Editorial Porrua, 1984.
"The Legal Practice."

878. Aragones Cucala, Manuel Y Ezequiel Tomas Biosca. <u>Manual de Derecho Positivo Mexicano</u>. 2a ed. Mexico: Editorial Patria, 1981.
"Handbook of Mexican Positive Law."

879. Brinsmade, L.L. "Mexican Law: An Outline and Bibliography of English Source Materials Relating to Certain Aspects Thereof". <u>The International Lawyer</u> 6 (October 1972): 829-857.

880. <u>Doing Business in Mexico</u>. Editor Susan K. Lefler. Albany: Matthew Bender, 1981.
Loose-Leaf Service.

881. Gutierrez Aragon, Raquel y Rosa Maria Ramos Verastegui. <u>Esquema Fundamental del Derecho Mexicano</u>. 9a ed. Mexico: Editorial Porrua, 1990.
"Fundamental Outline of Mexican Law."

882. Herget, James E and Jorge Camil. <u>An Introduction to the Mexican Legal System</u>. Buffalo: L.W.S. Hein, 1978.

883. Kozolchyk, Boris. "Mexico's Political Stability, Economic Growth and the Fairness of Its Legal System." <u>California Western International Law Journal</u> 18 (Winter 1987): 105-117.

884. Mexico: The Legal System: Selected
     Readings. Gainesville: University of
     Florida, 1981.

885. Moto Salazar, Efrain. Elementos de
     Derecho. 31a ed. Mexico: Editorial
     Porrua, 1985.
     "Elements of the Law."

886. Perry, F. V. "Understanding the Mexican
     Attorney: Legal Education and the
     Practice of Law in Mexico." The
     International Lawyer 10 (January 1976):
     167-179.

887. Ramirez Sanchez, Jacobo. Introduccion al
     Estudio del Derecho y Nociones de
     Derecho Civil. 2a ed. Mexico: UNAM,
     1987.
     "Introduction to the Study of Law and
     Notions of Civil Law."

888. Villoro Toranzo, Miguel. Introduccion al
     Estudio del Derecho. 8a ed. Mexico:
     Editorial Porrua, 1988.
     "Introduction to the Study of Law."

889. Weisbaum, Earl [et al.]. "Mexican Law
     for Norteamericanos: A Panel." Law
     Library Journal 68 (November 1975): 395-
     420.

State Material

AGUASCALIENTES

890. Codigo Civil (1947).
Civil Code.

891. Codigo de Procedimientos Civiles (1947).
Civil Procedure Code.

892. Codigo Penal y de Procedimientos Penales
(1949).
Criminal Code and Criminal Procedure
Code.

893. Ley del Notariado (1947).
Notary Law.

BAJA CALIFORNIA

894. Codigo de Procedimientos Civiles (1977).
Civil Procedure Code.

895. Codigo Penal y de Procedimientos Penales
(1977).
Criminal Code and Criminal Procedure
Code.

BAJA CALIFORNIA SUR

None

CAMPECHE

896. Codigo Civil (1943).
Civil Code.

897. Codigo de Procedimientos Civiles (1942).
Civil Procedure Code.

898. Codigo Penal (1974).
Criminal Code.

899. Codigo Penal de Procedimientos Penales (1975).
Criminal Procedure Code.

900. Ley del Notariado para el Estado de Campeche.
Notary Law for the State of Campeche.

CHIAPAS

901. Codigo Civil (1938).
Civil Code.

902. Codigo de Procedimientos Civiles (1938).
Civil Procedure Code.

903. Codigo de Procedimientos Penales (1936).
Criminal Procedure Code.

904. Codigo Penal (1938).
Criminal Code.

905. Constitucion Politica del Estado de Chiapas (1982).
Political Constitution of the State of Chiapas.

906. Ley de Hacienda para el Estado de Chiapas (1988).
Treasury Law of the State of Chiapas.

907. Ley de Ingresos para el Estado de
     Chiapas para el Ejercicio Fiscal 1989
     (1988).
     Law of Income for the State of Chiapas
     for the 1989.

908. Ley de Justicia Administrativa del
     Estado de Chiapas (1989).
     Administrative Law of the State of
     Chiapas.

909. Ley de Presupuesto, Contabilidad y
     Gastos Publico del Esatado de Chiapas
     (1990).
     Budget, Accounting and Public Expenses
     Law of the State of Chiapas.

910. Ley de Responsabilidades de los
     Servidores Publicos del Estado de
     Chiapas (1989).
     Civil Service Law of the State of
     Chiapas.

911. Ley del Notariado (1948).
     Notary Law.

912. Ley Organica de la Administracion
     Publica del Esatdo de Chiapas (1988).
     Organic Law of the Public
     Administration.

913. Ley Organica Municipal del Estado de
     Chiapas (1988).
     Organic Municipal Law of the State of
     Chiapas.

914. Ley Organica del Poder Judicial del
     Estado de Chiapas (1989).
     Organic Law of the Judiciary of the
     State of Chiapas.

CHIHUAHUA

915. Codigo de Defensa Social (1971).
Criminal Code.
916. Codigo de Procedimientos Civiles (1974).
Civil Procedure Code.

917. Codigo de Procedimientos en Materia de
Defensa Social (1971).
Criminal Procedure Code.

918. Codigo Municipal para el Estado de
Chihuahua (1982).
Municipal Code for the State of
Chihuahua.

919. Ley Organica del Poder Judicial (1989).
Organic Law of the Judiciary.

COAHUILA

920. Codigo Civil (1941).
Civil Code.

921. Codigo de Procedimientos Civiles (1941).
Civil Procedure Code.

922. Codigo de Procedimientos Penales (1982).
Criminal Procedure Code.

923. Codigo Penal (1982).
Criminal Code.

924. Constitucion Politica (1918).
Political Constitution.

925. Ley de Hacienda (1978).
Treasury Law.

926. Ley de Desarrollo Urbano (1977).
Urban Development Law.

927. Ley Estatal de Organizaciones Politicas
y Procesos Electorales (1979).
State Law on Political Organizations and
Electral Process.

928. Ley Organica de la Administracion Public
(1980).
Organic Law of the Public
Administration.

929. Ley Organica de la Administracion
Publica Municipal (1981).
Organic Law of the Municipal Public
Administration.

930. Ley Organica del Poder Judicial (1940).
Organic Law of the Judiciary.

931. Reglamento Interior del Congreso (1940).
Regulations of the Congress.

COLIMA

932. Codigo Civil (1953).
Civil Code.

933. Codigo de Procedimientos Civiles (1954).
Civil Procedure Code.

934. Codigo de Procedimientos Penales (1955).
Criminal Procedure Code.

935. Codigo Penal (1955).
Criminal Code.

936. Constitucion Politica (1917).
Political Constitution.

937. Ley de Hacienda (1981).
Treasury Law.

938. Ley de Desarrollo Urbano (1976).
Urban Development Law.

939. Ley Organica del Poder Ejecutivo (1968).
Organic Law of the Executive.

940. Ley Organica del Poder Judicial (1955).
Organic Law of the Judiciary.

941. Ley Organica Municipal (1979).
Municipal Organic Law.

942. Reglamento del Registro Publico de la
Propiedad (1937).
Regulations of the Public Registry of
Property.

943. Reglamento Interior del Congreso (1972).
Regulations of the Congress.

DURANGO

944. Codigo Civil (1948).
Civil Code.

945. Codigo de Procedimientos Civiles (1948).
Civil Procedure Code.

946. Codigo Penal (1983).
Criminal Code.

947. Codigo Procesal Penal (1985).
Criminal Procedure Code.

GUANAJUATO

948. Codigo Civil (1965).
Civil Code.

949. Codigo de Procedimientos Civiles (1934).
Civil Procedure Code.

950. Codigo de Procedimientos Penales (1959).
Criminal Procedure Code.

951. Codigo Penal (1978).
Criminal Code.

952. Constitucion Politica (1917).
     Political Constitution.

953. Ley de Desarrollo Urbano (1977).
     Urban Development Law.

954. Ley de Hacienda (1979).
     Treasury Law.

955. Ley Organica del Poder Ejecutivo (1980).
     Organic Law of the Executive.

956. Ley Organica del Poder Judicial (1977).
     Organic Law of the Judiciary.

957. Ley Organica Municipal (1968).
     Municipal Organic Law.

958. Reglamento para el Gobierno Interior del
     Congreso (1945).
     Internal Regulations of the Congress.

GUERRERO

959. Codigo Civil (1937).
     Civil Code.

960. Codigo de Procedimientos Civiles (1937).
     Civil Procedure Code.

961. Codigo de Procedimientos Penales (1937).
     Criminal Procedure Code.

962. Codigo Penal (1953).
     Criminal Code.

963. Codigo del Menor (1956).
     Code for Minors.

964. Constitucion Politica (1917-1918).
     Political Constitution.

965. Ley de Desarrollo Urbano (1976).
     Urban Development Law.

966. Ley de Hacienda (1982).
     Treasury Law.

967. Ley del Divorcio (1939).
     Divorce Law.

968. Ley del Notario (1979).
     Notary Law.

969. Ley Organica del Municipio Libre (1974).
     Municipality Organic Law.

970. Ley Organica del Poder Ejecutivo (1982).
     Organic Law of the Executive.

971. Ley Organica del Poder Judicial (1977).
     Organic Law of the Judiciary.

972. Ley Sobre el Regimen de Propiedad y
     Condominio (1956).
     Property and Condominium Law.

973. Reglamento del Registro Publico de la
     Propiedad (1980).
     Regulations of the Public Registry of
     Property.

974. Reglamento Interior del Congreso (1955).
     Regulations of the Congress.

HIDALGO

975. Codigo Civil (1940).
     Civil Code.

976. Codigo de Procedimientos Civiles (1940).
     Civil Procedure Code.

977. Codigo Fiscal del Estado de Hidalgo
     (1984).
     Tax Code of the State of Hidalgo.

978. Codigo Fiscal Municipal (1986).
     Municipal Tax Code.

979. Codigo Penal (1970).
     Criminal Code.

980. Codigo Procesal Penal (1970).
     Criminal Procedure Code.

981. Constitucion Politica del Estado (1920).
     Political Constitution of the State.

982. Ley de Asentamientos Humanos y
     Desarrollo Urbano (1977).
     Law of Population Center and Urban
     Development.

983. Ley de Hacienda (1981).
     Treasury Law.

984. Ley Organica de la Administracion
     Publica (1981).
     Organic Law of the Public
     Administration.

985. Ley Organica del Poder Judicial (1982).
     Organic Law of the Judiciary.

986. Ley Organica del Poder Legislativo
     (1982).
     Organic Law of the Legislature.

987. Ley Organica Municipal (1980).
     Organic Municipal Law.

988. Ley de Organizaciones Politicas y
     Procesos Electorales (1979).
     Law of Political Organizations and the
     Electrol Process.

989. Reglamento de la Ley de Organizaciones
     Politicas y Procesos Electorales (1980).
     Regulations of the Law of Political
     Organizations and the Electrol Process.

JALISCO

990. Codigo Civil (1935).
Civil Code.

991. Codigo de Procedimientos Civiles (1938).
Civil Procedure Code.

992. Codigo de Procedimientos Penales (1934).
Criminal Procedure Code.

993. Codigo Penal (1933).
Criminal Code.

994. Ley de Hacienda (1989).
Treasury Law.

995. Ley de Ingreso (1989).
Law of Income.

996. Ley Organica del Poder Ejecutivo (1989).
Organic Law of the Executive.

997. Ley Organica del Supremo Tribunal de
Justicia (1978).
Organic Law of the Supreme Court of
Justice.

MEXICO

998. Codigo Civil (1956).
Civil Code.

999. Codigo de Procedimientos Civiles (1937).
Civil Procedure Code.

1000. Codigo de Procedimientos Penales (1961).
Criminal Procedure Code.

1001. Codigo Penal (1986).
Criminal Code.

MICHOACAN

1002. Codigo Civil (1936).
      Civil Code.

1003. Codigo de Procedimientos Civiles (1964).
      Civil Procedure Code.

1004. Codigo Penal (1980).
      Criminal Code.

1005. Codigo Procesal Penal (1980).
      Criminal Procedure Code.

MORELOS

1006. Codigo Civil (1945).
      Civil Code.

1007. Codigo de Procedimientos Civiles (1955).
      Civil Procedure Code.

1008. Codigo de Procedimientos Penales (?).
      Criminal Procedure Code.

1009. Codigo Penal (1945).
      Criminal Code.

1010. Constitucion Politica (1931).
      Political Constitution.

1011. Ley de Desarrollo Urbano (1980).
      Urban Development Law.

1012. Ley de Hacienda (1977).
      Treasury Law.

1013. Ley Organica de la Administracion Public
      (1981).
      Organic Law of the Public
      Administration.

1014. Ley Organica del Congreso (1979).
      Organic Law of the Congress.

1015. Ley Organica del Poder Judicial (1980).
Organic Law of the Judiciary.

1016. Ley Organica Municipal (1981).
Organic Municipal Law.

NUEVO LEON

1017. Codigo Civil (1935).
Civil Code.

1018. Codigo de Procedimientos Civiles (1973).
Civil Procedure Code.

1019. Codigo de Procedimientos Penales (1984).
Criminal Procedure Code.

1020. Codigo Penal (1981).
Criminal Code.

1021. Ley de Aparceria (1940).
Sharecropping Law.

1022. Ley Que Regula el Condominio de
Edificios (1955).
Law that Regulates Condominium
Buildings.

1023. Ley Reglamentaria del Registro Publico
de la Propiedad y del Comercio (1972).
Regulatory Law of the Public Registry of
Property and Commerce.

OAXACA

1024. Codigo Civil (1943).
Civil Code.

1025. Codigo de Procedimientos Civiles (1944).
Civil Procedure Code.

1026. Codigo de Procedimientos Penales (1979).
Criminal Procedure Code.

1027. Codigo Penal (1979).
Criminal Code.

1028. Constitucion Politica (1922).
Political Constitution.

1029. Ley de Expropiacion (1950).
Expropriation Law.

1030. Ley del Notariado (1953).
Notary Law.

1031. Nueva Ley Organica del Poder Judicial
(1954).
New Organic Law of the Judiciary.

PUEBLA

1032. Codigo Civil (1985).
Civil Code.

1033. Codigo de Defensa Social (1943).
Criminal Code.

1034. Codigo de Procedimientos Civiles (1986).
Civil Procedure Code.

1035. Codigo de Procedimientos en Materia de
Defensa Social (1943).
Criminal Procedure Code.

1036. Constitucion Politica (1917).
Political Constitution.

1037. Ley de Ejecucion de Sanciones Privativas
de la Libertad (1975).
Law of Execution of Sanctions that
Deprive One of Liberty.

1038. Ley de Expropiacion (1924).
Expropriation Law.

1039. Ley Organica del Departamento Judicial (1943).
Organic Law of the Judiciary.

QUERETARO

1040. Codigo Civil (1951).
Civil Code.

1041. Codigo de Procedimientos Civiles (1950).
Civil Procedure Code.

1042. Codigo de Procedimientos Penales (1931).
Criminal Procedure Code.

1043. Codigo Penal (1931).
Criminal Code.

1044. Ley del Regimen de la Propiedad en Condominio (1973).
Law of Condominium Property.

1045. Ley Reglamentaria del Registro Publico de la Propiedad (1954).
Regulatory Law of the Public Registry of Property.

1046. Ley Sobre el Arrendamiento (1971).
Law on Leasing.

QUINTANAROO

1047. Codigo Civil (1980).
Civil Code.

1048. Codigo de Procedimientos Civiles (1980).
Civil Procedure Code.

SAN LUIS POTOSI

1049. Codigo Civil (1946).
Civil Code.

1050. Codigo de Procedimientos Civiles (1947).
Civil Procedure Code.

1051. Codigo Penal (1984).
Criminal Code.

1052. Ley Sobre el Regimen de Propiedad y
Condominio de los Edificios Divididos en
Pisos, Departamentos, Viviendas e
Locales (1976).
Condominium and Property Law.

SINALOA

1053. Codigo Civil (1940).
Civil Code.

1054. Codigo de Procedimientos Civiles (1940).
Civil Procedure Code.

1055. Codigo de Procedimientos Penales (1939).
Criminal Procedure Code.

1056. Codigo Penal (1939).
Criminal Code.

1057. Ley del Instituto de Proteccion a la
Infancia (1975).
Law of the Institute for the Protection
of Children.

1058. Ley Organica de Consejo Tutelar para
Menores (1980).
Organic Law of the Guardianship Council
for Minors.

1059. Ley Sobre el Regimen de Propiedad y
Condominio (1972).
Property and Condominium Law.

1060. Reglamento del Registro Civil (1982).
Regulations of the Civil Registry.

SONORA

1061. Codigo Civil (1949).
Civil Code.

1062. Codigo de Procedimientos Civiles (1949).
Civil Procedure Code.

1063. Codigo de Procedimientos Penales (1949).
Criminal Procedure Code.

1064. Codigo Fiscal (1977).
Tax Code.

1065. Codigo Penal (1949).
Criminal Code.

1066. Ley de Ejecucion de Sanciones Privativas
y Medidas Restrictivas de Libertad
(1972).
Law of the Execution of Sanctions
Depriving One of Freedom.

1067. Ley de Hacienda (1980).
Treasury Law.

1068. Ley Electoral para el Estado de Sonora
(1987).
Electoral Law of the State of Sonora.

1069. Ley Sobre el Regimen de Propiedad y
Condominio de los Edificios Divididos en
Pisos (1957).
Property and Condominium Law.

TABASCO

1070. Codigo Civil (1950).
Civil Code.

1071. Codigo de Procedimientos Civiles (1950).
Civil Procedure Code.

1072. Codigo de Procedimientos Penales (1948).
Criminal Procedure Code.

1073. Codigo Penal (1972).
Criminal Code.

TAMAULIPAS

1074. Codigo Civil (1961).
Civil Code.

1075. Codigo de Procedimientos Civiles (1961).
Civil Procedure Code.

1076. Codigo de Procedimientos Penales (1956).
Criminal Procedure Code.

1077. Codigo Penal (1956).
Criminal Code.

1078. Ley Sobre el Regimen de Propiedad y
Condominio (1965).
Property and Condominium Law.

TLAXCALA

1079. Codigo Civil (1976).
Civil Code.

1080. Codigo de Procedimientos Civiles (1980).
Civil Procedure Code.

1081. Codigo de Procedimientos Penales (1979).
Criminal Procedure Code.

1082. Codigo Penal (1979).
Criminal Code.

VERACRUZ

1083. Codigo Civil (1932).
Civil Code.

1084. Codigo de Procedimientos Civiles (1932).
      Civil Procedure Code.

1085. Codigo de Procedimientos Penales (1948).
      Criminal Procedure Code.

1086. Codigo Penal (1980).
      Criminal Code.

1087. Ley de Ejecucion de Sanciones (1947).
      Execution of Sanctions Law.

1088. Ley Sobre el Regimen de Propiedad y
      Condominio de los Edificios Divididos en
      Pisos, Departamentos, Viviendas o
      Locales (1956).
      Property and Condominium Law.

YUCATAN

1089. Codigo Civil (1942).
      Civil Code.

1090. Codigo de Defensa Social (1987).
      Criminal Code.

1091. Codigo de Procedimientos Civiles (1942).
      Civil Procedure Code.

1092. Codigo de Procedimientos en Materia de
      Defensa Social (1987).
      Criminal Procedure Code.

1093. Codigo del Registro Civil (1942).
      Civil Registry Code.

1094. Ley del Notariado (1939).
      Notary Code.

1095. Ley Sobre el Regimen de Propiedad y
      Condominio Inmobilario (1972).
      Property and Condominium Law.

1096. Reglamento del Registro Publico de la
Propiedad (1941).
Regulations of the Public Registry of
Property.

ZACATECAS

1097. Codigo Civil (1986).
Civil Code.

1098. Codigo de Procedimientos Civiles (1965).
Civil Procedure Code.

1099. Codigo de Procedimientos Penales (1966).
Criminal Procedure Code.

1100. Codigo Penal (1966).
Criminal Code,

Notes

1. See generally Guillermo Floris Margadant, <u>An Introduction to the History of Mexican Law</u> (Dobbs Ferry, N.Y.: Oceana Publications, 1983); also Toribio Esquival Obregon, <u>Apuntes para la Historia del Derecho en Mexico</u> (Memorandum on the History of the Law in Mexico), 2nd ed. (Mexico: Editorial Porrua, 1984).

2. See generally Fernando Flores Garcia, "La Administracion de Justicia en los Pueblos Aborigenes de Anahuac" (The Administration of Justice in the Aborigen Towns of Anahuac), <u>Revista de la Facultad de Derecho de Mexico</u> 15 (Enero-Marzo 1965): 81; also Lucien Biart, <u>The Aztecs: Their History, Manners, and Customs</u> (Chicago: A.C. McClure and Company, 1887); also Lucio Mendieta y Nunez, <u>Derecho Precolonial</u> (Precolombian Law), 5th ed. (Mexico: Editorial Porrua, 1985).

3.   Jose Maria Ots Capdequi, <u>Manual de
     Historia del Derecho Espanol en las
     Indias: Y del Derecho Propiamente
     Indiano</u> (Handbook of the History of the
     Laws of Spain in the the Indies: And of
     the Laws Exclusively of the Indies)
     (Buenos Aires: Editorial Losada, 1947),
     233.

4.   See generally Francisco Avalos, "The
     Legal Personality of the Colonial Period
     of Mexico," <u>Law Library Journal</u> 83
     (Spring 1991): 393-400.

5.   James E. Herget and Jorge Camil, <u>An
     Introduction to the Mexican Legal System</u>
     (Buffalo, N.Y.: William S. Hein, 1978),
     6.

6.   Ots Capdequi, supra note 3, 78.

7.   Avalos, supra note 4, 396.

8.   Ibid., 399.

9.   Herget, supra note 5, 4.

10. See generally, supra note 1; also
     Octavio A. Hernandez and Miguel Angel
     Porrua, eds., <u>Derecho del Pueblo
     Mexicano: Mexico a Traves de Sus
     Constituciones</u> (Rights of the Mexican
     Nation: Mexico Through its
     Constitutions), 3rd ed. (Mexico: Camara
     de Diputados, 1985).

11. Herget, supra note 5, 7.

12. John Henry Merryman, <u>The Civil Law
     Tradition: An Introduction to the Legal
     Systems of Western Europe and Latin
     America</u>, 2nd ed. (Stanford, California:
     Stanford University Press, 1985), 15.

13. Margadant, supra note 1, 189.

14. Ibid., 223.

15. See generally Richard D. Baker, <u>Judicial Review in Mexico: A Study of the Amparo Suit</u> (Austin: University of Texas Press, 1971).

16. <u>Enciclopedia de Mexico</u> (Encyclopedia of Mexico), 4th ed., s.v. "constituciones" (constitutions).

17. <u>Constitution of the United Mexican States</u> (1917), Title 1, Chapter 1, Section 1, Paragraph A.

18. Miguel de la Madrid Hurtado, <u>Estudios de Derecho Constitucional</u> (Constitutional Law Studies) 3rd ed. (Mexico: Editorial Porrua, 1986), 104.

19. Alberto Trueba Urbina, <u>The Mexican Constitution of 1917 Is Reflected in the Peace Treaty of Versailles of 1919</u> (New York: s.n., 1974), 104.

20. Madrid Hurtado de la, supra note 18, 113.

21. Ibid., 113.

22. Merryman, supra note 12, 24.

23. <u>Constitution of the United Mexican States</u> (1917), Title 2, Chapter 1, Article 40.

24. Ibid., Chapter 1, Article 39.

25. Ibid., Chapter 2, Article 43.

26. Ibid., Chapter 1, Article 41.

27. Ibid., Chapter 2, Article 43.

28. E.V. Niemeyer, <u>Revolution at Queretaro: The Mexican Constitution Convention of 1916-1917</u> (Austin: University of Texas Press, 1974) 228.

29. Madrid Hurtado de la, supra note 18, 114.

30. Niemeyer, supra note 28, 134.

31. Ibid., 234.

32. Ann M. Bartow, "The Rights of Workers in Mexico," <u>Comparative Labor Law Journal</u> 11 (Winter 1990): 182.

33. Madrid Hurtado de la, supra note 18, 189.

34. Herget, supra note 5, 31.

35. Ibid., 31.

36. <u>Constitution of the United Mexican States</u> (1917), Title 6, Article 123, Section 14.

37. Ibid., Section 18.

38. Ibid., Section 9, Subsection A through F.

39. Herget, supra note 5, 32.

40. <u>Constitution of the United Mexican States</u> (1917), Title 3, Chapter 1, Article 49, Paragraph 2.

41. Vincent L. Padgett, <u>The Mexican Political System</u>, 2nd ed. (Boston: Houghton Mifflin Company, 1976), 192.

42. Herget, supra note 5, 20.

43. Padgett, supra note 41, 198.

44. Constitution of the United Mexican States (1917), Title 3, Chapter 2, Section 4, Article 78.

45. Herget, supra note 5, 19.

46. Padgett, supra note 41, 200.

47. Ibid., 200.

48. Constitution of the United Mexican States (1917), Title 3, Chapter 4, Article 94.

49. Ley Organica del Poder Judicial de la Federacion (Organic Law of the Federal Judiciary), (1981).

50. Constitution of the United Mexican States (1917), Title 3, Chapter 4, Article 98.

51. Ibid., Article 96.

52. Ibid., Article 94, Paragraph 2.

53. Paul Berstein, "El Derecho y el Hecho: Law and Reality in the Mexican Criminal Justice System," Chicano Law Review 8 (1985): 55.

54. Constitution of the United Mexican States (1917), Title 3, Chapter 4, Article 97, Paragraph 1.

55. Ibid.

56. Ibid., Articles 103, 104, 105, 106, 107.

57. Herget, supra note 5, 72.

58. Constitution of the United Mexican
     States, (1917), Title 3, Chapter 4,
     Article 107. Also Ley de Amparo
     ("Amparo" Law) (1935).

59. See generally Baker, Supra note 15.

60. Helen L. Clagett and David M.
     Valderrama, A Revised Guide to the Law
     and Legal Literature of Mexico
     (Washington, D.C.: Library of Congress,
     1973), 38.

61. Herget, supra note 5, 28.

62. Clagett, supra note 60, 221.

63. Frederic Meyers, Mexican Industrial
     Relations from the Perspective of the
     Labor Courts (Los Angeles: Institute of
     Industrial Relations, 1979), 30.

64. See generally Diccionario Juridico
     Mexicano (Mexican Legal Dictionary), 2nd
     ed., s.v. "Tribunales Militares"
     (Military Courts).

65. See generally Merryman, supra note 12.

66. Ibid., 6.

67. Ibid., 11.

68. Ibid., 13.

69. Ibid., 14.

70. Ibid., 6.

71. Ibid., 13.

72. Thomas H. Reynolds and Arturo A. Flores, <u>Foreign Law: Current Sources of Codes and Legislation in Jurisdictions of the World</u> (Littleton, Colorado: Fred B. Rothman & Company, 1989), Mexico 1.

73. Merryman, supra note 12, 60.

74. Ibid., 16.

75. Berstein, supra note 53, 45.

76. Merryman, supra note 12, 18.

77. <u>Constitution of the United Mexican States</u> (1917), Title 3, Chapter 4, Article 107, Section 2 and 13. Also Ley de Amparo ("Amparo" Law) (1935).

78. See generally Victor Vilaplana, "Mexican Law for Norteamericanos," <u>Law Library Journal</u> 68 (November 1975): 396-399.

79. See generally Ezequiel Guerrero Lara, <u>Manual para el Manejo del Semanario Judicial de la Federacion</u> (Manual for the Use of the Judicial Weekly of the Federation) (Mexico: Instituto de Investigaciones Juridicas, 1982).

80. Guerrero Lara, supra note 79, 13.

81. Ibid., 13.

Appendix: Directory of Publishers

PUBLISHERS, ADDRESSES

Ediciones Andrade, S.A.
Colima Numero 213
APDO. Postal 24-351
Mexico (7), D. F.
Ediciones Andrade offers 14 Loose-Leaf
Services which together will cover all of the
major laws, regulations, decrees, etc. that
you might need.

Editorial Porrua
Av. Republica Argentina 15
Mexico 1, D. F.
Editorial Porrua's Leyes y Codigos de Mexico
Collection offers 38 titles that will cover
all of the major laws, regulations, decrees,
etc. that you might need.

Hispanic Books Distributor, INC.
1665 West Grant Road
Tucson, Arizona 85745
(602)882-9484
Hispanic Books Distributor can secure any
title you may need. They have an especially
close relationship with Editorial Porrua.

They also provide books from the other Latin American Nations. The owner is a retired Professor of Library Science which makes for easier communications.

Mexico Sur/Norte.
P.O. Box 1682
Redlands, CA 92373
(714)793-7842
Mexico Sur/Norte can obtain for you the "Diario Oficial de la Federacion," and the Mexican State "Diarios". They also can provide the paperback federal and state codes published by Porrua. Mexico Sur/Norte is very willing to work with you on a personal basis to better meet your special needs.

Puvill Libros, S.A.
Puvill Mexican Division
Empresa 109
Colonia Mixcoac
Mexico, D.F. 03910
Puvill handles many Mexican publishers and is a good source for primary and secondary materials.

Author Index

(Numbers refer to entry numbers)

Subject Index

(Numbers refer to entry numbers)

About the Author

FRANCISCO A. AVALOS, Foreign Law and International Law Librarian, College of Law, University of Arizona, also teaches courses on foreign and international law librarianship at the Graduate Library School. He is also the author with Arturo L. Torres of *Latin American Legal Abbreviations: A Comprehensive Spanish/Portuguese Dictionary with English Translations*, Greenwood Press, 1989.